SHEDS in CAMERA

SHEDS in CAMERA

John Hooper

Oxford Publishing Co.

Plate 1: The massive shearlegs of Neasden Shed are made ready to lift Class D11 'Director' 4-4-0 No. 5507 *Gerald Powys Dewhurst* in order to fit a new set of front driving wheels which, as can be seen, have the bearing surfaces wrapped for protection whilst they were in transit from Gorton Works. Shearlegs were a feature to be seen outside most of the larger LNER running sheds, and both stout timber and the later steel types, with hand or electric winding gear, were common at the ex-GCR sheds. Elsewhere, different profiled types, including hydraulically-assisted designs, served other ex-company sheds. The advent of wheel drops sited inside the sheds away from the elements, must have made the fitting staff a happier lot.

British Rail

ISBN 0 86093 324 5

A FOULIS-OPC Railway Book

© 1984 J. Hooper & Oxford Publishing Co.
Reprinted 1986 & 1989

Published by:
Haynes Publishing Group
Sparkford, Near Yeovil, Somerset. BA22 7JJ

Haynes Publications Inc.
861 Lawrence Drive, Newbury Park, California 91320, USA.

Printed by: J. H. Haynes & Co. Ltd

Introduction

There have been many books written about the London & North Eastern Railway and its main constituents, the Great Central, Great Eastern, Great Northern, Great North of Scotland, North Eastern and the North British railways, but none of these books have really ventured to describe or show, photographically, the less glamorous side of these railway companies' locomotive operations, the locomotive running shed. This volume contains 303 photographs of 125 separate locations, which are intended to give the reader an insight into the LNER engine sheds during the period when that company existed, in the days prior to its formation, as well as the period after nationalisation.

The first part of the book covers the building of new engine sheds by the LNER, during the period when the company was under financial stress in the 1930s. Following, is the section dealing with locomotive servicing, and all that it entailed. The LNER, of course, was quick to grasp the fact that modern, up to date methods of servicing meant that locomotives could spend more time hauling trains and earning revenue, due to the drastic cuts achieved in servicing time at the sheds. Shortly after the Grouping, the first huge concrete coaling plants were being planned for the busiest 'sheds' or, as they later became known, 'depots'. Government loans in the 1930s enabled the company to furnish many more sites with mechanical servicing plant, and so it entered World War II with just enough plant to help keep the locomotives running during a period of manpower shortage and extremely heavy traffic.

The shed buildings themselves were a huge collection of various standard pre-grouping designs, some in good condition and others, usually the small non-standard shed, in a run-down dilapidated condition with hardly any room to accommodate their allocation. The North Eastern Railway was a roundhouse builder or, more correctly, a square roundhouse builder, while the Great Northern Railway sheds were straight road affairs with hipped or 'northlight' roofs. The North British Railway standardised the transverse-pitched roof for their larger sheds whilst the Great North of Scotland Railway had no standard design to talk of, the Great Eastern Railway employing straight road buildings with 'northlight' or multi-bay pitched roofs. The Great Central Railway, being the youngest company had, of course, inherited the Manchester, Sheffield & Lincolnshire sheds which were usually of the 'northlight' type, a design chosen as standard for the London Extension Railway engine sheds. All these different shed types are included in this book, together with many photographs of the smaller sheds, while locomotive material has been included to help the reader digest the shed views.

The final section of the book deals with the sheds after they were closed to the steam locomotive. Some went on to serve private industry while some, even to this day, serve British Rail in one form or another. Perhaps the most fitting end came to two of the York roundhouses, which were chosen to house the National Collection, at what is now the National Railway Museum. Most sheds suffered the final indignity of demolition and their sites, once cleared, give no clue at all of the hustle and bustle, smoke and grime, the atmosphere and, dare I say it, the 'magic' of the shed, be it known as a locomotive running shed or motive power depot.

John Hooper,
Shaw,
Oldham,
1984

1 Elgin
2 Keith
3 Banff
4 Macduff
5 Fraserburgh
6 Peterhead
7 Boat of Garten
8 Inverurie
9 Alford
10 Kittybrewster
11 Aberdeen Ferryhill
12 Ballater
13 Montrose
14 Arbroath
15 Dundee Tay Bridge
16 Tayport
17 St Andrews
18 Mallaig
19 Fort William
20 Arrochar
21 Aberfoyle
22 Perth
23 Ladybank
24 Loch Leven
25 Thornton Junction
26 Methil
27 Anstruther
28 Dunfermeline
29 Burntisland
30 Stirling
31 Alloa
32 Kinniel
33 Polmont
34 Bathgate
35 Kipps
36 Haymarket
37 St Margarets
38 Penicuik
39 Helensburgh
40 Balloch
41 Lennoxtown
42 Eastfield
43 Stobcross
44 Kilsyth
45 Parkhead
46 Longniddry
47 North Berwick
48 Dunbar
49 Peebles
50 Galashiels
51 Duns
52 St Boswells
53 Kelso
54 Jedburgh
55 Hawick
56 Riccarton Junction
57 Carlisle Canal
58 Silloth
59 Tweedmouth
60 Alnmouth
61 Rothbury
62 Reedsmouth
63 North Blyth
64 South Blyth
65 Percy Main
66 Heaton
67 Gateshead
68 Bowes Bridge
69 Blaydon
70 Hexham
71 Alston

72 Wearhead
73 Consett
74 Pelton Level
75 Borough Gardens
76 Tyne Dock
77 Sunderland
78 Durham
79 Middleton in Teesdale
80 Penrith*
81 West Auckland
82 West Hartlepool
83 Haverton Hill
84 Stockton
85 Newport
86 Saltburn
87 Guisborough
88 Darlington
89 Kirkby Stephen
90 Leyburn
91 Hawes
92 Northallerton
93 Whitby
94 Pickering
95 Scarborough
96 Bridlington
97 Malton
98 Pateley Bridge
99 Starbeck
100 York
101 Ilkley
102 Neville Hall
103 Copley Hill
104 Bradford
105 Ardsley
106 Normanton *
107 Selby
108 Cudworth
109 Barnsley
110 Hull Dairycoates
111 Hull Springhead
112 Hull Botanic Gardens
113 Hull Alexandra Docks
114 Southport
115 Walton-on-the-Hill
116 Brunswick
117 Bidston
118 Widnes
119 Wigan
120 Trafford Park
121 Gorton
122 Heaton Mersey
123 Chester Northgate
124 Wrexham
125 Northwich
126 Dinting
127 Hayfield
128 Darnall
129 Mexborough
130 Doncaster
131 Frodingham
132 Immingham
133 Louth
134 Staveley
135 Retford GN
136 Retford GC
137 Langwith
138 Tuxford
139 Lincoln
140 Annesley
141 Derby Friargate
142 Colwick

143 Leicester GN
144 Leicester GC
145 Newark
146 Grantham
147 Sleaford
148 Boston
149 Spalding
150 Bourne
151 Stamford
152 New England
153 March
154 Wisbech
155 South Lynn
156 Kings Lynn
157 Hunstanton
158 Swaffham
159 Dereham
160 Melton Constable
161 Wells
162 Cromer Brach
163 Norwich City
164 Norwich Thorpe
165 Wymondham
166 Yarmouth Beach
167 Yarmouth Vauxhall
168 Yarmouth South Town
169 Lowestoft
170 Woodford
171 Aylesbury
172 Huntingdon East
173 Ely
174 Cambridge
175 Bury St Edmunds
176 Stowmarket
177 Laxfield
178 Framlingham
179 Aldeburgh
180 Ipswich
181 Felixstowe Beach
182 Parkeston
183 Walton
184 Clacton
185 Colchester
186 Kelvedon
187 Sudbury
188 Braintree
189 Thaxted
190 Saffron Walden
191 Hitchin
192 Buntingford
193 Bishops Stortford
194 Ware
195 Hertford East
196 Hatfield
197 Enfield Town
198 Epping
199 Ongar
200 Chelmsford
201 Brentwood
202 Maldon
203 Southminster
204 Palace Gates
205 Wickford
206 Southend
207 Wood Street
208 Hornsey
209 Kings Cross
210 Neasden
211 Spitalfields
212 Canning Town
213 Stratford

* LMS Shed

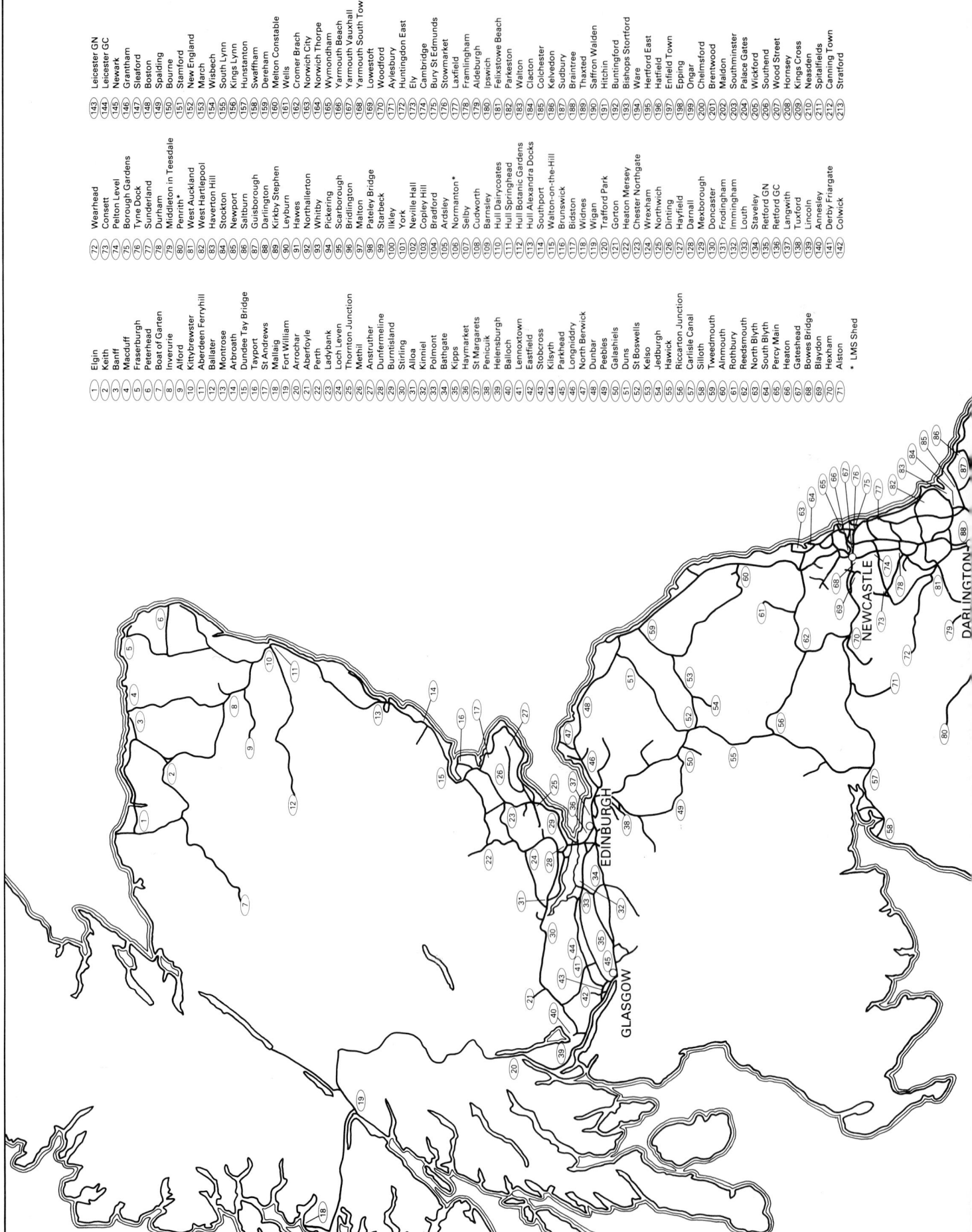

NEW AND REBUILT SHEDS

The iron and steel producing complex at Appleby-Frodingham was one of the largest in Western Europe. With the increasing appetite of the local blast furnaces for iron ore from Highdyke, and other raw materials that were railborne, the LNER decided that a locomotive running shed would be better placed in the centre of this complex, rather than carry on with the arrangement of providing motive power from the sheds at Doncaster and Keadby, both some distance to the west of Scunthorpe, and entailing excessive light engine working to and from the steelworks sidings. A plan, drawn up in the late 1920s, provided for a five road through type engine shed to be sited at Frodingham, measuring 250ft. x 75ft. It would be equipped with all the latest aids to serve and repair an allocation expected to consist of some thirty large freight locomotives, and a number of small engines used for shunting duties. The following photographs show the various stages of construction of the shed and its facilities during the early years of the 1930s.

Plate 2:   The massive monolithic foundations needed for the shed and engine pits, are evident in this May 1931 photograph which shows the amount of work and materials used before the engine shed proper could be erected.

BR/OPC Collection

Plate 3: Once the footings had been built up to the required height, tip waste was dropped into the void, as is witnessed in this May 1931 view looking at the engine pits at the west end of the shed. Those that can be seen in the background have steel reinforcing bars for the walls, sprouting up on each side.

BR/OPC Collection

Plate 4: The office, mess-room and workshop accommodation section of the shed did not require the same type of foundation as the engine roads but, nevertheless, these pier type stilts were needed to ensure stability. This August 1931 view shows a completed section awaiting the ground fill.

BR/OPC Collection

Plates 5 & 6: Two views of the turntable pit being prepared in May 1931.

BR/OPC Collection

Plate 7: Even the ash pit, which was some distance to the east of the new shed, required huge foundations as high as 25ft. to bring them to the new level, and thousands of tons of fill was required to level the yard.

BR/OPC Collection

In the first photograph, a sign reads:

FRODINGHAM ENGINE DEPOT
WEST END ELEVATION OF SHED.
31·12·31. — 3670.

Plate 8: The western end of the nearly-completed shed, on New Year's Eve 1931, with a smattering of seasonal snow on the ground.

BR/OPC Collection

Plate 9: An interior view of the shed, showing details of the roof construction. The main roof supporting girders were about to be clad in concrete.

BR/OPC Collection

FRODINGHAM ENGINE DEPOT
INTERIOR OF ENGINE SHED

FRODINGHAM ENGINE DEPÔT.
ELEVATIONS FROM SOUTH-WEST.
31·12·31 ———— 3671.

Plate 10: With newly-laid track in the yard and detailed constuction work proceeding, the shed is taking shape but is still some months from completion. The exaggerated 'westernlight' roof was an old but trusted design, and was much favoured by the LNER design staff.

BR/OPC Collection

Plate 11: The completed shed, fitted with roller shutter doors, awaits an allocation of locomotives in May 1932.

W. A. Brown Collection

Plates 12 & 13: Frodingham Shed, some fifteen years after completion, showing the effects of the atmospheric conditions on the concrete from the surrounding steelworks environment, as well as the resident steam locomotives.

BR/OPC Collection

Plate 14: In April 1943, the LNER brought into use a new locomotive depot at Darnall, in the City of Sheffield. The site for this new depot was chosen in 1936 as it was then apparent that the old ex-MS&LR engine shed at Neepsend, some distance to the west, was cramped, in need of repair and was unable to expand to accommodate its allocated 100 plus locomotives. The new shed was built during the early war years, and incorporated a 'westernlight' roof in a double-ended ten road design. A two road machine and fitting shop, complete with a wheel drop and hoist, was entered from the eastern end of the yard, while a coaling plant, a 200ft. long wet ash pit and a 70ft. turntable completed the locomotive facilities. The 750 strong staff had the rare privilege of new messrooms, kitchen, locker rooms and even a refrigerator, while a dormitory with fifty beds was built at the south-west corner of the site. This view of the western end of the depot, taken in May 1943, shows two roads leading from the bottom of the picture. The left-hand one is the incoming road, where locomotives arriving on shed from the west would have first crossed over the four track main line via a specially-built flyover. On entering the depot area, engines would first proceed to the turntable or use the bypass road if turning was not necessary. Next the coaling plant was visited, then the water-column and finally the ash pit, before backing on to one of the shed stabling roads. Just to the left of the picture, space can be seen for where the planned four road electric locomotive servicing shed was to be built. In the event, only a two road shed was required, and then it was nearly a decade before it was erected.

BR/OPC Collection

Plate 15: The eastern end of Darnall Locomotive Depot, as seen by the official photographer in May 1943. The two road repair shop is on the left of the main building, whilst the tall structure in the centre of the picture contains a 100,000 gallon water tank, complete with a pitched roof.

BR/OPC Collection

Plate 16: Although the negative is damaged, this view of Whitemoor Yard Engine Shed is included because it records the virtually spotless new building only two months after opening, on Boxing Day 1932. The five road shed was classified as a 'wash-out' shed, although most of its clientele were locomotives working in and out of the adjacent marshalling yards and requiring a quick service and turn round. Being near to to one of the country's large brick-making areas, the new shed was built from that most common of materials, unlike Frodingham and Thornton sheds which were built at the same time. A 'northlight' roof, clad in asbestos sheeting, was used to top the structure, and yard facilities included a 70ft. vacuum-operated turntable, a coaling plant, an ash disposal plant plus adequate stabling roads, all of which were shared with the adjacent March Engine Shed, which was sited just to the south. The need for this extra engine shed was brought about by the expansion and modernisation of the marshalling yard of the same name (then the largest in Britain), sited on either side of the main line to the north.

BR/OPC Collection

FACILITIES

Plate 17: Ardsley coaling stage, as seen by the official photographer before the Grouping, with private-owner as well as company coal wagons on the ramp. Built for the opening of the shed in 1892, the stage was superseded in later years by a mechanical coaling plant. On the extreme right of the picture, alongside the Class J52 0-6-0, is the sand drying house with its many assorted chimneys, whilst next to the ramp, in the foreground, is the yardmen's shack or 'bothy'.

National Railway Museum

Plate 18: The small, yet robust, coaling stage at the former MS&L shed at Keadby, near Scunthorpe, circa 1930. Although a shelter was provided, the height and exposed position must have presented a few problems for the gang of coalmen when the weather was foul, and the wooden ladder is evidently ready for the fire.

W. A. Brown Collection

Plate 19: Piecemeal repairs had obviously been carried out to Bathgate coaling stage over the years and, in this 1965 view, the structure looks ready to 'give up the ghost'. Two coaling chutes were originally in use but in later years, only the chute furthest from the camera was used. Twelve months after this scene was photographed, the stage became redundant with the closure of Bathgate Shed.

A. A. Maclean

Plate 20: The coaling stage at Leicester Depot (ex-Great Central Railway) was of a standard design that could also be found at other depots built for the London Extension Railway. Here two Class A5 4-6-2T locomotives are being refuelled whilst the crew of No. 5158 pose for the camera, and staff from the adjacent sand furnace house look on. The coaling stage, brought into use with the opening of the depot in 1898, was topped with a 75,000 gallon capacity water tank. This type of stage was very similar to examples found on the LNWR and LYR, but the raised coaling road on the GCR type was usually about 12ft. above yard level instead of those other companies' more usual 6ft.

BR/OPC Collection

Plate 21: A pre-grouping photograph of the large single-sided coaling stage at Eastfield Engine Shed in Glasgow. The stage was built in 1904 ready for the opening of the new NBR depot in September of that year. Although disused from the early 1930s, because of the building of a large 500 ton capacity mechanical coaling plant, the stage was left standing, although redundant, until the advent of BR. This was in case of breakdown of the coaling plant which, at a large depot like Eastfield, could have disastrous results without an alternative method of refuelling engines.

A. G. Ellis

Plate 22: Class 04 2-8-0 No. 6269 (later 63781) waits in line with another member of the same class, to replenish its tender with coal at Staveley stage in 1931. Each of the wooden-sided 'loco' coal wagons on the elevated ramp held 20 tons of black diamonds, and on these stages every pound of coal was manhandled with shovels from the wagons into small four-wheeled tubs. These, in turn, were tipped on the platform (seen between the locomotives' chimneys) into the waiting, ever hungry tenders. At some of the busier engine sheds, as many as ten or more wagons would be emptied during every shift. Many of these installations were in use until the end of steam on BR, but the LNER, along with the LMS and SR, built a large number of mechanical coaling plants to supersede them. An exception was the GWR, which kept on with this old method of refuelling, involving sweat, toil and dirt galore for the coaling gang.

G. Coltas

Plate 23 (above): In the BR period of steam locomotive working, coal stacks were rarely found at depots, but prior to World War II massive coal stacks, built up like solid dry stone walls, could be found at most sheds. Coal being the lifeblood of railways in the pre-diesel/electric era, companies bought and stored as much of the precious commodity as money and space would allow, just in case of shortages. In this view, we see just two of the many stacks built up by the GER at Stratford Shed.

National Railway Museum

Plate 24 (below): As it was situated far away from the major coalfields, and because it was not a major carrier of the stuff, the GER was prone to any coal shortages that might occur. Thus in this picture, a gang of men can be seen breaking into one of Stratford's prized stacks and loading the open wagons ready for movement to the coal stage. In our day of mechanisation, this time consuming and energy sapping exercise seems almost soul destroying.

National Railway Museum

Plate 25: The huge double-sided coaling stage at New England, was one of the largest structures in the land built solely for replenishing the bunkers of steam locomotives. This view, in late March 1965, was taken after the 'official' closure of New England Shed, but Class B1 No. 61272 is alongside in the guise of Departmental No. 25. Just in front of the stage is the sand house which, again, is a large building, befitting a depot of this size, and behind on the right can be seen part of the coaling plant of LNER vintage. At many of the larger LNER sheds, the old coaling stages were kept in situ, when space permitted, in case of mechanical breakdown of the more modern appliance.

W. Potter

Plate 26: Class J10 0-6-0 No. 5839 is seen being coaled at the Heaton Mersey (Cheshire Lines Committee) coaling stage in June 1935. This stage closely follows a Midland Railway design, and the double-sided loading arrangement meant that each of the two main companies involved at this shed, the GCR and the MR, had separate coaling facilities, with each company staying to its own side of the stage. This was a rule that also stood in the running shed, off the picture and to the right. After the Grouping these arrangements were kept going for a while, although pooling became necessary during the war years and the years leading up to nationalisation.

W Potter

Plate 27: Coaling cranes were to be found at many of the smaller engine sheds, and this example was sited at Pickering. The date of installation is not known, but it was most probably of North Eastern Railway origin.

G. S. Lloyd

Plate 28 (left): The small 1 ton capacity mechanical coaling plant at King's Cross locomotive yard, photographed in August 1931, with Class N2 0-6-2T No. 2671, (later No. 69577) receiving a load of fuel whilst the fireman looks on, probably for the official photographer's benefit. A number of these smaller coaling appliances were erected at running sheds by the LNER but this one, although installed after the Grouping, was ordered by the GNR.

BR/OPC Collection

Plate 29: The 70ft. high reinforced concrete coaling plant at King's Cross 'Top Shed', pictured when nearing completion. This design, with a 500 ton bunker capacity, was very similar to other plants erected for the LNER during the late 1920s and early 1930s, at the larger depots such as Doncaster, Gorton, March, Neville Hill and New England. Coaling plants of this type usually cost around £8,000 to build and the erection was always carried out by a specialist company, with Henry Lees & Co. and Mitchell Conveyors getting the bulk of the contracts from the LNER.

Photomatic

Plate 30: Henry Lees & Co. Ltd. built the mechanical coaling plant at Kittybrewster during 1932, when the same company supplied many coaling plants to the LNER. This plant did not have the standard outline of the other concrete monoliths erected during this period, and a wagon hoist was also included instead of the more usual skip hoist. Another claim to fame was that this was the most northerly coaling plant on the LNER system.

W. H. Whitworth

Plate 31: The 250 ton capacity, electrically-operated twin bunker coaling plant at Darnall was able to refuel a locomotive tender with eight tons of coal in less than three minutes. Coal was loaded into the bunkers via a skip hoist which, when filled by a wagon tippler at ground level, would be hoisted to the top of the plant where its contents, depending on the grade of coal, would be tipped into either of the bunkers.

BR/OPC Collection

Plate 32 (below): The designer of the 250 capa-city coaling plant at Cambridge must have thought he had some sort of artistic license, judging by the amount of concrete blisters on the superstructure of the tower. This coaler was brought into opera-tion in 1932, along with other modifications to the former GER shed layout and facilities. Class J15 No. 65438 was one of five members of its class fitted with a tender cab for working the Colne Valley line, and is seen here at 31A in August 1953.

B. Morrison

Plate 33:   The 500 ton capacity coaling plant at York (North) was built by Mitchell Engineering Co. to one of their own designs for the LNER, and was ready for use by 1932. The pre-war view, looking south towards the main locomotive yard, also shows the old coaling stage on the right, which was superseded by this modern appliance.

Author's Collection

Plate 34 (above): Gorton coaler, as seen by the cameraman in May 1935.

Bill Potter

Plate 35 (above): Although the 500 ton capacity mechanical coaling plant at Whitemoor had been in operation for only a few months before this May 1928 photograph was taken, it was already sporting a thick coating of coal dust. This was a nuisance that could be partly alleviated by thoroughly wetting a wagon load of coal before it was hoisted to the top of the plant and discharged into the bunker. Here, a 20 ton steel-sided wagon is about to ascend the 70ft. tower.

BR/OPC Collection

Plate 36 (left): A close up of the safety grids covering the wet ash pit at Darnall. This 200ft. long pit was 10ft. deep, contained about 6ft. of water and could hold about one week's quota of ash and clinker. For emptying the pit, a grab crane was employed during any quiet periods. This type of ash disposal plant had been installed at various depots by the LNER from the early 1930s, and was an efficient way of dealing with the nuisance of dust and the sometimes non-apparent danger of piles of ash.

BR/OPC Collection

Plate 37: Class 02/4 No. 63935, looking as grubby as its surroundings, stands on one of the ash pit roads at New England Shed in May 1959. It will be noticed that the cages normally covering the pit have been removed, probably to allow removal of debris from the pit by the grab crane. At some depots, though, the cage retaining lugs had, over the years, been broken off, leaving the pit open and therefore dangerous for the unwary.

B. Morrison

Plate 38: The wheel drop at Frodingham was supplied by Ransomes & Rapier of Ipswich, a well-established railway equipment supplier. Wheel drops made the work of the fitting staff a somewhat more comfortable occupation than did the shearlegs of pre-grouping origin which, at most engine depots on the LNER, were sited outside the sheds. The apparatus for working the wheel drop is just to the right of the workshop door, this particular type being electrically-operated, whereas earlier models were hydraulically-powered.

BR/OPC Collection

Plate 39 (above): No. 63843, undergoing major surgery at Langwith Junction in May 1965. The scale of repairs carried out at so late a date seems surprising, but it must be remembered that the shed fitters were trying to keep in traffic, ancient and worn out locomotives which no longer had a 'main' works to visit. Therefore, rather than condemn a still useful and much-needed revenue earner, lengthy repairs such as this were carried out.

W. A. Brown

Plate 40 (above): A typical ex-North British Railway water-column, complete with a small specially-designed stove strapped to its waist, and with an exhaust ascending the full height of the column. The harsh winters experienced north of the border necessitated measures such as this, whereas further south, railway companies made do with a portable brazier for cold weather protection. This example was photographed at Polmont.

A. A. Maclean

Plate 41 (left): The machine shop at Darnall was to be equipped with new machine tools for its opening in 1943 but, because of wartime shortages, the old machines from Neepsend had to be retrieved and brought in for a new lease of life.

BR/OPC Collection

Plate 42:   The 7,500 gallon a minute capacity water softening plant at Retford (ex-GNR) Shed was one of dozens scattered about the LNER system. This softener was erected in 1934, and the water supply pipes can be seen bridged across to the shed's overhead supply tank, which dated from 1875. Behind the Shell-BP oil tank wagons can be seen the sludge carriers, converted redundant locomotive tenders, that were used to transport the by-product of the water softening process.

BR/OPC Collection

Plate 43:   The messroom of Colwick (ex-GNR) Depot in October 1944, obviously emptied of staff for the benefit of the official photographer because, at a large shed such as this, there was always someone taking a break. This was one of the better messrooms to be found at any engine shed or in any railway company, and was built as part of the modernisation scheme carried out at Colwick from 1936 onwards.

BR/OPC Collection

Plates 44 & 45: To instruct its enginemen and shed staff in the working of the steam locomotive and the various valve gears etc., the LNER provided an instruction train which toured the running sheds of the Southern Area of the railway, staying at the sheds from two up to ten days at a time, depending on the number of men stationed there. In this November 1944 view, taken at Hatfield Shed, the train was made up of an ex-GER twelve-wheeled saloon and a former GCR luggage van. The lower view shows the inside of the GCR van, fitted out as a lecture theatre complete with models and diagrams, with the GER saloon carrying most of the major full size exhibits used for instruction.

BR/OPC Collection

Plate 46: At the west end of Gateshead Shed, in 1954, Class J25 No. 5658 could be found in use as the depot's stationery boiler. This locomotive came here in 1949 after being withdrawn from Northallerton (51J), but that shed's code can still be seen on the smokebox. It wasn't unusual to find withdrawn engines, that still had sound boilers, carrying out this mundane duty although, in most cases, boilers would be found grounded on a brick plinth. When the tender of this locomotive needed refuelling it was detached from the engine and hauled off to the coaling stage which, in this case, required the shed pilot engine to haul it through three of the depot's four roundhouses before access to the yard was gained. The water supply was less of a problem, as a fixed hydrant was sited adjacent to a water-column, just out of the picture to the left.

B. Morrison

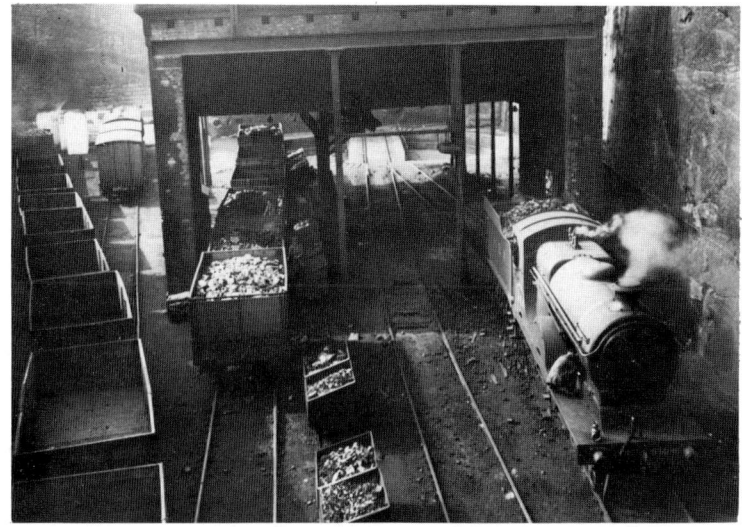

Plate 47: Finally, for this section reviewing the facilities, we have a view of Brunswick (CLC) in July 1937, showing the cramped layout of the servicing area which was sited between the shed on the left and the sandstone cutting, which was hewn out to accommodate the depot in the mid-1800s. The small 'Lynn' type coaling plant was, as can be seen, built beneath the water tank of the original coaling stage, a location that was surely unique for this country. Coal tubs running on 2ft. gauge track can be seen in abundance, whilst beyond is the 60ft. turntable. This type of location is the answer to many modellers' problems of siting an engine depot, as it can be tucked away in the corner of most layouts. Class D9 4-4-0 No. 5104 *Queen Alexandra* completes the satanic scene.

W. Potter

THE BREAKDOWN TRAIN

Following the sequence of *LMS Sheds in Camera*, a review of the London & North Eastern Railway's breakdown trains and cranes is made here. This is to show some of the equipment at the disposal of that Company's breakdown gangs who were, of course, drawn from the ranks of the running shed staff. A more complete picture of the allocations of LNER steam breakdown cranes is given in *LNER Wagons* by Peter Tatlow, but for a more detailed insight of the cranes themselves, J. S. Brownlies book *Railway Steam Cranes* is an invaluable source of information. The nine views depicted here show some of the steam cranes inherited by the LNER from its constituents, cranes purchased by the company and some of the many that went on to serve British Railways after nationalisation.

Plate 48: A Stratford breakdown train, circa 1910, with two four-wheeled vans for the crew and stores and a 20 ton capacity steam crane, all headed by Class M15 2-4-2T No. 183. Both the locomotive and the crane were built in 1908 at the Stratford Works of the Great Eastern Railway. The engine later became LNER Class F4 No. 7183 and was withdrawn in 1934 whereas the crane, numbered 4A by the GER, served the LNER and BR for a total of 58 years at sheds such as Ipswich and March, being displaced from Stratford, just before the Grouping, by a 35 ton capacity crane.

National Railway Museum

Plate 49: This 36 ton capacity steam breakdown crane was delivered from Cowans, Sheldon & Co., in 1914, to the North British Railway at a cost of £3,290. The crane was stationed at St. Margaret's from new, and spent the next 48 years there until it was reallocated to Thornton Junction in 1962. Closure of that shed in 1967 saw the appliance moved to Dundee, where it resided in the ex-Caledonian engine shed. Numbered 770517 by the NBR, the crane gained the LNER number 971567 in 1938 although, at nationalisation, BR (Scottish Region) renumbered the crane to RS 1062/36, following the old LMS scheme adopted by that region. It is seen here at the back of Dundee Shed in 1970. In November 1978 the crane was withdrawn, and is now preserved at Falkirk.

J. Templeton

Plate 50: The first steam breakdown cranes purchased by the LNER were two 45 ton capacity units, supplied by Cowans, Sheldon & Co. in 1926. Virtually identical in detail, with an unusual double bogie design, the cranes had a very limited route availability, but as they were introduced purely to attend to any incidents involving the growing number of Pacifics in use on the LNER main line, this factor did not matter. One was numbered 22, which spent all its life at Gateshead Shed until withdrawn in 1968, while No. 39A, seen in this superb close up view, was allocated to Doncaster Shed. It left there in 1968 as BR No. 330107, and was reallocated to Healey Mills.

BR/OPC Collection

Plate 51: Purchased in 1939, from Cowans, Sheldon & Co. of Carlisle, this 45 ton capacity steam crane was the first of six similar cranes delivered from the same firm during 1940. This machine was originally allocated to Thornton Junction but, within a few months, had moved to Eastfield where it was to stay. Fitted with detachable relieving bogies, the crane was able to work over any part of the system even though its weight was nearly 100 tons. Numbered 971588 by the LNER, it became No. RS 1058/45 under BR, and is seen here in its stabling position, on the main line side of Eastfield Depot.

J. Templeton

Plate 52: The 35 ton capacity Cambridge steam breakdown crane No. SB5, photographed in February 1933, shortly after delivery from the makers, Ransomes & Rapier of Ipswich. This machine spent all of its working life on the Great Eastern Section, serving at Norwich and Stratford before being withdrawn in March 1970.

BR/OPC Collection

Plate 53: The Eastfield breakdown train in 1921, with the locomotive crew posing with the breakdown gang. It will be seen from the photograph that the crane just about fits the NBR loading gauge. The new engine shed makes a fine backdrop having barely been completed, and much of the brickwork has yet to be stained by engine exhausts.

Scottish Record Office.

Plate 54: Inherited from the North Eastern Railway, this latticed jib 35 ton capacity steam crane served the LNER until nationalisation when, while stationed at Thornton Junction, it became No. RS 1063/35 and, before withdrawal in 1967, was reallocated to Aberdeen (Ferryhill) and later Perth. It cost the NER £3,020, in 1912, when it was delivered new from the makers, Craven Bros. of Stockport, to York Shed. In 1927 it was sent to Eastfield where it served for thirteen years before moving to Thornton Junction in 1940. LNER numbers in order were 770569, 971569 and 971580. Prior to the Grouping it carried the number CME 15, and was one of seven steam breakdown cranes operated by the NER.

J. Templeton

Plate 55: On the NBR section of the LNER, breakdown cranes were put to good use even when they were not required to attend mishaps. This is illustrated by the splendid scene of the Thornton 20 ton capacity crane, No. 770539, lifting Class J35 No. 9375 (later 64505) to extract its rear driving wheels, at the old shed, circa 1929. The crane, of NBR origin, was acquired in 1882 from the Glasgow firm of Forrest & Co. and was allocated to Cowlairs Running Shed, later moving to the new shed at Eastfield. In 1927, Thornton was blessed with its presence and once again, in 1933, it was moved across to the larger more modern depot which opened that year at Thornton. Duties such as that depicted here were not required at the new shed, as the said establishment was equipped with a wheel drop, but, when required, it did travel to Bathgate and Polmont to carry out this routine task. The year 1940 saw the crane transferred to Bathgate as No. 972571, then in 1947 to Kipps, and after nationalisation to Dalry Road as No. RS 1051/18, its BR designation. Withdrawal came in September 1964 and its original high purchase price of £1,210, some 82 years previously seems, in the end, to have been a bargain. It will be noticed that none of the three outriggers are in use, as this was an end-on straight lift, but rail clamps can be seen below the buffers.

B. Hilton Collection

Plate 56: Another Cowans, Sheldon & Co. 45 tonner, acquired by the LNER in 1940, was this unit allocated to Cambridge Shed as No. 961606, seen here in 1970, while still serving British Rail as No. 330133. It was usual to have a siding or stabling road set aside for the breakdown train, where coal could be stacked and water hydrants were available, as the crane was kept in steam ready to be called out to any incident. On the right can be seen the breakdown gang's travelling van and, at the front of the train, packing and tool vans. This kind of make-up has been in use since the earliest days of breakdown trains.

P. Tatlow

TURNTABLES

Plate 57: New livery, new owners, new site and new turntable. Former GCR Class 9P 4-6-0 *Lord Stuart of Wortley*, tests out the recently installed 70ft. diameter manual turntable at King's Cross Station Shed Yard, shortly after the Grouping.

F. Moore

Plate 58: Scarborough's 50ft. turntable was placed at the north end of the shed yard, and on this day in 1933 was loaded with resident 'Hunt' class D49 *The Zetland*.

D. J. Montgomery

Plate 59: Hardly a testing load for the new 70ft. diameter 165 ton capacity turntable, installed for the opening of Frodingham Shed, but the official photographer would make do with any locomotive as long as it was reasonably clean. Thus with the crew posing, Class J50 No. 1063 (later BR 68963) makes its mark in railway history in September 1932.

BR/OPC Collection

Plate 60: Grace and power are combined in this unnamed Class A1 Pacific No. 60150, seen on the 70ft. vacuum-operated turntable at Haymarket in August 1949.

D. J. Montgomery

Plate 61 (right): The 70ft. diameter vacuum-operated articulated turntable at Darnall, featuring Class V2 No. 4865, specially polished for the official photographer one month after the opening of the facilities.

BR/OPC Collection

Plate 62 (left): Class D20 No. 2014 is turned on the outside 50ft. turntable in the yard of Hull (Botanic Gardens) Shed, circa 1939.

D. J. Montgomery

Plate 63 (right): With Grantham Station in the background, Class C1 Atlantic No. 4439 turns on the 70ft. turntable at Grantham in 1931. This turntable was installed at the start of Pacific workings on the East Coast Main Line and was, for many years, one of the manual types.

G. Coltas

Plate 64: Even when a Class A4 locomotive is balanced properly on a turntable, moving its 160 ton bulk through 180 degrees by manpower alone can be a struggle. This was certainly true for these men at Eastfield in April 1949, with Haymarket's No. 60011 *Empire of India*. Shortly after this trial of strength, a vacuum tractor was fitted to the 70ft. turntable.

V. Forster

Plate 65: Electric-powered turntables required no effort from crew or yard staff, except for the manipulation of a small handle. This view of the turntable at York (North) shows the driver of the world speed record holder, No. 60022 *Mallard*, nonchalantly standing by as he starts the turning sequence to get his charge facing the right way to work back to the Capital.

W. A. Brown

Plate 66: Darlington acquired this 70ft. turntable during the period when the straight shed was renewed at the start of World War II. The table was one of the examples fitted with vacuum cylinders, fitted on both sides of the platform. Here, ex-works Class B16 No. 61433, with its 52ft. 6in wheelbase, has plenty of room to spare.

V. Forster

Plate 67: King's Cross Station Shed turntable again, this time with one of the more usual residents, in the form of Class A1 Pacific No. 4474 *Victor Wild*, complete with mirror like finish in 1927.

W. J. Reynolds

Plate 68: The 70ft. diameter articulated turntable at Dunfermline, photographed shortly after installation in 1951. These modern units had vacuum tractors fitted as standard, and the connection hose fitted to locomotives that had vacuum gear can be seen alongside the control cubicle. To enable non-vacuum locomotives to be turned, storage tanks were fitted on either side of the table and were, as in this view, very prominent. Steel plate decking was a feature of modern turntables, as opposed to the timber used on the older units, while the pit floor was constructed of concrete segments, which took the place of the circular brick layout of old installations.

British Rail

Plate 69: When three of the Great Eastern section 'Britannia' Pacifics were sent to the Southern Region of BR for evaluation in 1951, three of the Southern's 'Battle of Britain' Light Pacifics were transferred to Stratford to take their place. This October 1951 view illustrates No. 34057 *Biggin Hill*, complete with 30A Stratford shed plate, being turned on the 70ft. turntable at Ipswich.

H. N. James

Plate 70: Not all steam locomotive turntables were scrapped after the cessation of steam on British Railways, as this 55ft. diameter example at Leeds (Neville Hill) illustrates. Supplied by Cowans, Sheldon & Co. to the North Eastern Railway in 1900, it was luckily acquired for further use by the North Yorkshire Moors Railway preserved line in March 1975, and is seen here being dismantled prior to its move to the new location.

J. H. Meredith

THE SHEDS

Plate 71:   The shed foreman looks on as Class C11 4-4-2 No. 9872 *Auld Reekie* lives up to its name at Aberdeen (Ferryhill) in September 1930. This former Caledonian shed was, by this time, in the hands of the LMS but, due to long standing agreements, the LNER was able to stable and service its engines here as well as at Kittybrewster, on the north side of the city. At least one ex-NBR Atlantic was kept here to work the Dundee and Edinburgh trains, and the usual LNER presence here also included locomotives of Class D29, D30, J37, J38 and J39, as well as the larger Class 04s and assorted shunting engines.

G. Coltas

Plate 72: On the same day, Class C11 No. 9509 *Duke of Rothesay* gets last minute attention from a Ferryhill fitter before working south to its home shed of Dundee (Tay Bridge).

G. Coltas

Plates 73 & 74:   The NBR concern at Alloa consisted of this two road stone-built shed, dating from around 1885. In the upper view the rebuilt end of the shed can be seen, whilst the lower view shows the original stone arches of the front end, framed in the gantry of the coaling appliance. Both scenes were recorded on 2nd August 1953, and on shed that day were the usual mixture of NBR-designed goods and tank locomotives.

B. K. B. Green

Plates 75 & 76: Alnmouth Shed in July 1952, with one of Tweedmouth's Class J39 locomotives No. 64815. Sited on the west side of the junction of the East Coast Main Line and the Alnwick branch, Bilton Junction (as Alnmouth was first known) was built in 1875 and typical brick-arched entrances gave some clue to its NER origin. Facilities included a 42ft. diameter turntable and, as can be seen on the right, a raised coaling ramp equipped with two balanced tipping platforms to aid hand coaling. The shed survived until 1966 and, in the lower view, we see two of its 1964 allocation of six Class K1 2-6-0s.

A. G. Ellis & W. T. Stubbs

Plate 77: The branch to Alston diverged from the Carlisle to Newcastle main line at Haltwhistle and, after serving four intermediate stations, the train completed its journey at this handsome little terminus. After detaching from its train, the engine would pull forward on to a 42ft. 4in. diameter turntable and, after turning, would run through the 93ft. long engine shed to the water-column and afterwards, if need be, the coaling platform. Having cleaned the fire, the crew would then manoeuvre their charge on to the front of the train for the return working, or reverse the locomotive back into the shed if its day's work was complete. This view of Alston in 1950 shows the facilities very much intact, having stood for almost a century. During the BR period, Standard 2-6-0 tender locomotives worked the bulk of the passenger and freight traffic over the branch, but prior to this, LNER Class J21 and J39 tender and Class G5 and N8 tank locomotives found employment. The shed closed in September 1959 after diesel railcars took over the passenger service, but now even the branch itself has closed.

C. A. Appleton

Plate 78 (left): For a number of years it was the practice of the East Midlands Branch of the Railway Correspondence & Travel Society to run railtours using distinguished, if not unusual, engines for motive power. This photograph of 'Schools' class 4-4-0 No. 30925 *Cheltenham*, at Annesley Motive Power Depot in May 1962, shows cleaning being carried out by members of the RCTS prior to the event. The locomotive, incidentally, was chosen purely because it bore the name of the town where the Society was formed in the 1920s.

V. Forster Collection

Plate 79: The vast amount of ground area taken up by a medium-sized motive power depot, can be appreciated from this panoramic view of Annesley in June 1965. The actual engine shed occupied only a fraction of land, compared with the rest of the servicing and stabling area, and it must be realised that not all of the depot area is in view, as this photograph was taken from the coaling plant. On the left of the picture can be seen a group of tracks fanning out into what was once the coal stacking ground, empty by this time, as the authorities had decided to run down stocks, the depot having only six months of operational life left. The allocation of the former GCR shed at this time consisted of sixty odd engines, half of which were BR Standard Class 9F 2-10-0s, while the rest were ex-LMS 'Black Fives' and Class 8Fs. This was a far cry from ten years earlier when almost all of the seventy plus allocation was made up of ex-GCR-built locomotives with a few ex-GNR and LNER types thrown in. Standing in the heart of a vast coalfield, evidence of which can be clearly seen with a slag heap forming the backdrop, Annesley's principal work was to supply engines for local trip workings and long distance coal hauls. Opened in 1898, the shed was the first of the London Extension standard 'northlight' sheds, and had accommodation for thirty locomotives. Growth in coal traffic saw the allocation doubled by World War I, but the six road shed was never extended. The LNER carried out major improvements in the mid-1930s when a coaling plant was erected to supersede the manual coaling stage, seen here on the right when still intact. A water softener was supplied, and eventually extra stabling roads were laid but without any cover. A 65ft. diameter turntable has since taken the place of the 54ft. unit, which was sited where the grab crane now stands. All traces of this depot have now gone, although the coal traffic in the area still generates much of BRs income.

D. Swales

Plate 80: A close up of Annesley Shed, pictured when the Class 01 2-8-0 locomotives reigned in the 1950s.

Photomatic

Plate 81: About the only things that were clean at Ardsley in 1964 were the lamps adorning the various locomotives. The WD 2-8-0 engines were latecomers to this former GNR shed, arriving as late as 1960 to replace the Class J6 and J39 0-6-0s which had served the West Riding shed for so long. At least half a dozen engines of LMS origin were allocated during the BR period, most of them staying on the allocation list until closure in October 1965. The shed was rebuilt by BR in the early 1950s, its original 'northlight' roof being replaced by a variation of the standard louvre concrete roof.

A. George

Plate 82: The Great North of Scotland Railway engine shed at Ballater dated from 1893, and stood on the south side of the terminal station of the same name. As can be seen in this 1936 view, a four road carriage shed separated the two.

Plate 83: Typical motive power for the Ballater branch were the Class D41 locomotives of 4-4-0 wheel arrangement and of GNS origin. Here, No. 6912 (renumbered 2256) of Kittybrewster is seen outside the two road stone-built shed at Ballater, during the mid-1930s, refuelled and ready to work back to Aberdeen. A 50ft. diameter turntable was provided, with extension rails to 54ft., and the pit of the table is visible on the left.

W. L. Good

Plate 84:   Bathgate, as can be seen in this 1949 view, was a typical NBR standard shed, with transversed-pitched roofs and raised smoke vents. Opened in 1902, the six road shed was a dead end type and during most of its life housed 0-6-0 types of Class J35 and J36, with usually thirty or more of them amongst the forty plus allocation and, therefore, nothing more than a 50ft. diameter turntable was required right up to closure. The shed was completely rebuilt in 1954, and its outline changed dramatically with the use of asbestos corrugated cladding. The number of stabling roads was cut down to three, with a one road repair shop built on to the north side of the shed. Like so many others in Scotland, the depot closed in 1966.

W. Potter

Plate 85:   Very similar in design to the original NBR roundhouse at St. Margaret's in Edinburgh, the same company's engine shed at Berwick, opened during the 1840s, consisted of what could be termed as a semi or half-moon roundhouse, with only thirteen roads offering covered accommodation for locomotives. The building was certainly attractive and was, as far as LNER constituent companies went, both unusual and rare. Indeed, there were no more than a dozen examples of this kind of engine shed throughout the British Isles, and when it is realised that almost 2,000 sheds served the steam locomotive during its reign, comparisons can be made. This shed, standing at the southern extremity of the old NBR section of the East Coast Main Line, was closed just after the Grouping, and shortly afterwards was demolished to make way for station improvements. What remained of its locomotive stud was reallocated to the former NER shed at Tweedmouth, south of the Royal Border Bridge.

Scottish Record Office

Plate 86: The former GCR depot at Bidston, on the Wirral, in June 1936, with Class N5 0-6-2T No. 5915 simmering outside. The interior of the 'northlight' shed is clearly visible, mainly due to the whitewashed walls. The doors are still intact, which was a prevalent occurrence at the smaller LNER engine sheds until 1948. Notice also the ranks of rainwater downspouts on the left-hand walls, a peculiarity of 'northlight' sheds.

W. Potter

Plate 87: On 19th January 1958, Bidston was home for BR 2-10-0s (actually allocated to nearby Birkenhead) as well as visiting Class 04s from Gorton. By this time the shed roof had been rebuilt, and a small mechanical coaling plant enhanced the meagre facilities. The snowstorm gives the place an arctic atmosphere, and goes to prove the point that most railway enthusiasts rank with mountaineers and lone 'round the world' yachtsmen when it comes to braving the elements.

B. Hilton

Plate 88: Bidston, some four month later, and the weather has a hint of spring to it, although Class 04/1 2-8-0 No. 63719 of Gorton is in the autumn of its life, and has but a few years of service left before the cutter's torch dismantles it just a hundred yards away from its home shed.

N. Joseph

Plate 89: Borough Gardens, or at least part of the shed, in March 1950 with, from the left, Class J71 No. 68287, Class J72 No. 8679 and Class J71 No. 8289 gathered around one of the shed's four turntables. The first two tank engines not only carry new 54C shed plates on their smokebox doors, but they also have the legend 'Boro Gdns' painted on their buffers beams, a throw back from North Eastern Railway days.

J. H. Meredith

Plate 90: The remains of what was the former NER shed at Bowes Bridge, pictured in September 1951, eight years after a fire had destroyed the roof. Stabled in the ruins on this day were Nos. 69097 and 69100, the resident Class N10 0-6-2 tank engines. In 1954 a new shed was erected on the site, but the new shed itself saw only seven years of operational life before it was closed in 1962. To the left of the picture the base of the chimney which once served the boilers of the winding house from which Bowes Bridge Shed was fashioned in the 19th century can be seen.

B. K. B. Green

Plate 91: Two Class F3 2-4-2 tanks are pictured, well and truly coaled up, outside Braintree Shed during the 1930s. It was usual to see two tank engines at this location as well as an 0-6-0 goods tender engine, all locomotives being supplied by Colchester. The shed building was erected in 1910, replacing a similar structure that had been blown down in a gale the year before. A 45ft. turntable was sited some distance away, on the west side of Braintree Station, but the coaling facilities were primitive, with staff having to shovel coal from wagon to bunker.

W. A. Camwell

Plate 92: A summer Saturday scene at Bridlington, in the late 1950s, with the three road shed and its yard beginning to fill up with motive power from incoming excursion trains. All the engines on view are 'foreigners' including, on No. 1 road, a 'Crab'. The depot's own allocation at this time comprised five D49 'Shire' class locomotives and two Class G5 0-4-4 tank engines.

D. J. Montgomery

Plate 93: The GCR always had the greater share of locomotive facilities at Brunswick (CLC) Shed. Even in 1957, with the shed under London Midland Region control, the old GCR was still in evidence, as this view from the footbridge above the shed shows.

A. Sommerfield

Plate 94: BR took it upon themselves to rebuild Brunswick Shed in the mid-1950s and in this official photograph, taken in February 1957, we see the finished product. The new shed is cut back slightly from the original line of the two pitched roofs of CLC (MS&LR) origin.

British Rail

Plate 95: Yet another view of Brunswick from the iron footbridge, this time looking south at the approach road and the sheerlegs, in 1951, with the ubiquitous Class J11 0-6-0s in attendance.

J. A. Peden

Plate 96: Standing like an ancient monument in the Kingdom of Fife was Burntisland roundhouse, built from local stone and seen here in June 1933. This was only weeks before most of its allocation was disbanded and the depot demoted to a sub-shed status, this coming about with the opening of the new engine shed at Thornton Junction.

A. G. Ellis

Plate 97: The former GER locomotive shed at Bury St. Edmunds in May 1957, with Class J15 No 65420 waiting at the western end of the three road shed. The number of locomotives allocated here rarely exceeded twenty, even in the days prior to the Grouping, but right up until closure in 1959, ex-GER types were hanging on to form the bulk of the allocation.

B. K. B. Green

Plate 98: Carlisle (Canal) was one of two LNER engine sheds situated in the border town. The former NER shed at London Road was closed in 1933, and the dozen or so engines from there were transferred to this ex-NBR shed, boosting its allocation to sixty odd locomotives. In addition to the obvious large passenger engines of NBR origin the shed had, from 1928 onwards, an allocation of Class A3 Pacifics, an association that lasted virtually until closure of the shed in 1963. One engine, No. 2749 *Flamingo* (renumbered 60095) spent most of its working life at Carlisle (Canal) except for a few weeks in February 1929 when, after delivery from the 'Plant', it was used by Doncaster Shed for a number of running-in turns. The shed consisted of a stone-built square roundhouse with a 50ft. turntable, whilst alongside was a three road straight shed. For the use of the larger engines a 65ft. turntable was situated in the yard, and that can just be made out on the left of this July 1957 view of the shed and its facilities. In 1935, the LNER announced that a 200 ton capacity coaling plant, ash disposal facilities, wheel drop shed and increased staff accommodation were to be provided, all of which were supplied before the outset of World War II.

H. C. Casserley

Plate 99: The CLC shed at Chester (Northgate) was opened in 1874 to cater mainly for the MS&LR locomotives which worked from the town, and this view of the establishment, in April 1936, shows the inevitable Class C13 tank, a class long associated with this place. Locomotives on shed this day were as follows; Class J10 Nos. 5640 and 5850, Class C13 Nos. 5047, 5050, 5055 and 5455, Class J62 No. 5882, Class N15 No. 5519 and 5906 and, finally, Sentinel steam railcar No. 51909 *Waterloo*. In BR days, the shed housed a number of former LMS tank engines as well as BR Standard types, most of the former GCR engines having disappeared to Gorton scrapyard, although a couple of Class J10s hung on until closure in 1959.

W. A. Camwell

Plate 100:   The rebuilt shed at Chester (Northgate) in May 1952, as seen from a passing train. Neat coal stacks were not a feature of this depot.

D. Clayton

Plate 101:   With an allocation in excess of sixty engines during most of the LNER period, and a three road shed with hardly enough room for a dozen large tender engines, it was inevitable that overspill would be a regular occurrence at Colchester. This view of the sidings, just to the east of the shed in March 1937, shows a wealth of locomotives which worked the GER section. The tram locomotive, incidentally, was No. 7135.

W. A. Camwell

Plates 102 & 103:   Now you see it, now you don't! The roof at Colchester had disappeared by April 1922, apparently consumed by fire. Luckily, the official photographer had been at work recording progress on the new track layout and signal box during 1921/22, and these two views capture the shed with its original 'northlight' roof in September 1921, and with no roof just eight months later. The GER, of course, did not bother to build a new roof and so it was left to the LNER to provide the single-pitched affair, something that lasted until the end of steam on the former GER lines.

British Rail

Plate 104: An aerial view of Colwick Locomotive Running Shed from the south, circa 1930. The yard appears to be fairly empty, although the coaling stage (top centre) seems to be doing a brisk trade. The first engine shed was established here by the GNR in 1876, and is the four road twin-hipped roofed building nearest the turntable. In 1882 the eight road shed in the centre of the block was opened with the 'northlight' style of roof, although the tall two road lifting/fitting shop, built at the same time, retains the earlier hipped roof design. Further enlargements in 1896 saw another 'northlight' shed erected, this time with four roads, and this can be made out sand-wiched between the wagon shop on the left and the eight road running shed. An extensive modernisation programme was implemented by the LNER in 1936 when the depot, with an allocation of 200 plus engines, had £35,000 spent on, amongst other things, a new 70ft. vacuum-operated turntable, a mechanical coaling plant, a 260ft. long wet ash pit, and improved stores, office and messroom accommodation. In the 1950s the running sheds were reroofed, although the lifting shop retained its original cover along with the former wagon shop. The latter had been used as an oil and engine parts store since the late 1930s, when wagon repairs were transferred to the nearby ex-LNWR engine shed which had closed in 1932 for engine purposes. During the LNER period the depot was simply coded COL, but on entering BR ownership Colwick became known as 38A. It then became 40E in 1958 and finally 16B in 1966 when, under London Midland Region control, the shed was closed in December of the same year.

Nottinghamshire County Library Service

Plates 105 & 106: Two of Colwick's residents in 1932. No. 3122 *(above)*, one the huge Class R1 0-8-2 tank engines, is pictured outside the four road 'northlight' shed. No. 3965 *(below)*, is one of the more versatile Class J52 tanks, with the coaling stage forming the background.

G. Coltas

Plate 107: Ex-GCR locomotives were associated with Colwick from the Grouping, and many of these reliable Class 04 2-8-0s were allocated virtually up to closure of the depot. Behind Class 04/7 No. 63699 can be seen the lofty repair shop in original condition, whereas the engine shed roof had been rebuilt by the time this picture was taken in July 1955.

B. Morrison

Plate 108: No. 90000, one of Colwick's forty odd WD 2-8-0s, peers out of the gloom of the four road shed in 1955. The depot supplied motive power for the numerous coal trains originating from the Nottinghamshire Coalfield, and most of the 150 plus allocation consisted of freight type engines. In addition to three more WDs sharing the picture, a solitary Class B1 4-6-0, No. 61201, can also be seen on the right.

B. Morrison

Plates 109 & 110: Consett was opened in the winter of 1875, known then as Benfieldside, but later it took on the name of Blackhill, after the station just to the north, and eventually Consett. The shed carried on a fairly quiet existence with never more than half a dozen engines allocated to handle the passenger and local shunting work. However, World War II brought an upturn in traffic, with larger goods engines such as Class J26 0-6-0s coming on to the shed's books, these being replaced soon afterwards by Class Q6 0-8-0s. The traffic demands of the local steel industry brought another batch of Class Q6s, and the allocation in February 1947 was as follows; Class Q6 0-8-0s Nos. 3351, 3357, 3359, 3361, 3365, 3372, 3377, 3404, 3418, 3433, 3439 and 3455, Class N8 0-6-2Ts Nos. 9384 and 9394 and Class N9 0-6-2Ts Nos. 9411 and 9414. At about this time it was decided to provide a single road, brick-built extension, twice the length of the original shed, but virtually of the same profile and sited alongside. Coaling was carried out with a small steam crane mounted on a plinth in front of the old shed. The upper view shows the shed in its original state with Class J39 No. 1473 standing alone in late July 1939, whilst in the lower view we see the shed in BR days with Class Q6 0-8-0s overpowering the extended, although meagre, accommodation. Consett was coded 54D by British Railways, this changing to 52K in October 1958, and closure came in May 1965 when diesel traction took over the remaining duties.

C. A. Appleton & W. T. Stubbs

Plate 111: The GNR locomotive interests at Leeds were centred on Copley Hill or, to be more precise, in the triangle formed by the Wortley East, West and South Junctions. This view of the west end of the five road shed shows it as it was when rebuilt by BR in the early 1950s. Motive power at this time consisted of a dozen or more Class A1 and A3 Pacifics for use on main line passenger duties, with as many tank engines and a handful of 0-6-0s for local passenger and yard work.

D. J. Montgomery

Plate 112: Prior to World War II, GNR Atlantics were the mainstay of the shed's long distance passenger turns and in this view Class C1 Atlantic No. 3280 is seen, in May 1939, being coaled ready to haul the 'up' 'Queen of Scots'.

W. Potter

Plate 113: Cudworth Shed closed at the end of July 1951 as a result of declining traffic and nationalisation, its remaining duties being taken over by the nearby LMS-built engine shed at Royston. The former H&BR shed stood at what was virtually the western end of its parent system, in a maze of yards and colliery lines, and its mainly freight engine allocation hauled coal trains from the surrounding coalfield to Hull. The eight road dead end shed had brick walls, and was topped with a 'northlight' roof supported by timber trusses and cast-iron columns. A 60ft. turntable was available at the south end of the yard, and a crane was provided for coaling locomotives. In 1928 the LNER erected a 50 ton capacity mechanical coaling plant, small by later standards, but at that time being one of only a handful of such plants to be found on the LNER. The wooden shearlegs, shown on the left of the picture, were superseded by a steel girder set in the early 1930s, and this 1926 view also shows what was a regular occurrence at Cudworth, all the locomotives turned before stabling, so they were ready to work back to Hull the proper way, chimney first. At the Grouping there were just over thirty engines allocated here but, by January 1949, there were only ten engines on the books of 53E the shed's BR code. These were Class 04 2-8-0s Nos. 63620, 63667 and 63751, Class Q5 0-8-0s Nos. 63272 and 63332, Class J25 0-6-0s Nos. 65667, 65703 and 65714 and Class A7 4-6-2Ts Nos. 69771 and 69789. All trace of the shed and its associated yards are now gone.

B. Hilton Collection

Plate 114: Cudworth, on the eve of nationalisation, with half the shed roof gone and numerous wagons replacing the locomotives. This slightly blurred but, none the less, important picture gives a good view of the layout and facilities, which were little changed from the shed's opening.

G. Reeve Collection

Plates 115 & 116: Darlington Bank Top, as seen in August 1938, with the main shed building, fashioned from the old wagon repair shop in the 1880s, looking its age. It also bears a likeness to a beseiged regimental headquarters rather than a locomotive running shed. In the background to the right can be seen the 1865 roundhouse, which celebrated its centenary before closure in March 1966. The main shed was demolished shortly after this photograph was taken and, in the lower view, the skeleton of the new purpose-built seven road shed can be seen in the course of erection.

W. A. Camwell & G. Harrop

Plate 117 (right): Darlington, on 27th June 1964, with the coaling plant discernible through the smoke haze above the rebuilt shed.

W. T. Stubbs

Plate 118 (right): Sentinel No. 8142 of West Auckland, waits outside Darlington Shed repair shop for examination, in company with sister unit No. 8145 during the latter days of the LNER.

V. Forster

Plate 119 (below): Although this photograph shows, in the main, the locomotive works at Darlington (North Road) it also shows, on the right, one of the original Darlington roundhouses which were built by the NER before Bank Top became the main locomotive running shed at this railway town. The running department vacated the North Road site around 1903, and the two roundhouses were used until 1933 for housing engines on works visits. This circa 1931 picture shows LNER 'Hush-Hush' 4-6-4 locomotive No. 10000, alongside the coaling stage, in the works for one of its numerous visits, whilst in the foreground are turntables which are also in for repair.

W. H. Whitworth per W. A. Camwell

Plate 120: Grubby Class B16/1 No. 61477 of York, does nothing to enhance the untidy yard outside the eastern end of Darnall Shed in 1955. The corrugated iron roof cladding gives a clue to the shed's wartime origin.

B. Morrison

Plate 121: It is not pure LNER, but the 1,500 volts d.c. Bo-Bo electric locomotive, BR Class EM1 No. 26036, had its origins in the Gresley period of the LNER along with the shed in which it is stabled. This view inside Darnall Electric Servicing Depot, in August 1955, barely twelve months after it was opened, would have been possible ten years earlier had not World War II intervened and altered the MSW electrification plans. The two road shed was originally to have been a four road through building but BR, who revived the Trans-Pennine electrification scheme, decided in their wisdom that a smaller structure would suffice and, in the event, were proved to be right. The locomotive became a member of Class 76 but is now just a memory, along with the post-war modernisation scheme it was built to serve.

B. Morrison

Plate 122:   Dinting, in May 1954, and the driver of Class J11 No. 64332 watches intently as the tender of his charge is refilled with water from the adjacent parachute tank. Evidence of the MSW electrification can be seen, and it will be noticed that the overhead wires were stopped short of the water tank enabling life to go on as normal for the footplatemen, at least on the shed road. The former GCR locomotive depot is now, of course, the home of the Dinting Railway Centre, and scenes such as this are now common on the much-expanded site.

B. K. B. Green

Plate 123:   Class W1 4-6-4 No. 60700, stopped for repairs inside Doncaster Shed in late August 1954. The shed plate is clearly visible and is, of course, Doncaster's own code of 36A.

B. Morrison

Plate 124: Three pre-grouping companies, the GCR, GNR and NER, are represented by this assortment of engines stabled at the north end of Doncaster Shed in the early 1930s. The large twelve road through shed was opened in 1876 by the GNR, to replace a much smaller and rather cramped establishment sited on the west side of the station next to the 'Plant'. With over 100 engines allocated to Doncaster in the late 1860s, the call for the new engine shed became very apparent and work on the site at Carr started in late 1873, costing over £37,000 to complete. A two road lifting/repair shop, equipped with shearlegs, was built on to the east side of the running shed, access to this being gained from the south end of the yard, and slated hipped roofs were provided over all parts of the building including the office/mess accommodation. Prior to the erection of the massive 500 ton capacity coaling plant by the LNER, Doncaster had two manual coaling stages sited at either end of the nearly half mile long yard, and these were kept in situ, although disused, for a number of years until demolition. Further improvements carried out in the late 1920s and early 1930s included the installation of wet ash pits, sand hoppers and a 70ft. turntable.

Railway Photographs

Plate 125: Doncaster Motive Power Depot, on 31st August 1954, and ex-works Class J50/2 0-6-0T No. 68932 of Bradford stands below a macabre, but necessary, notice sited above No. 2 road. The notice reads 'To drivers, shunters, have you enquired if anyone is at work on these roads?'

B. Morrison

Plate 126: If only every engine shed yard could have been captured on film from a high vantage point like this. This is, of course, the north end of Doncaster Shed, as seen from the coaling plant in May 1935. Nothing more needs to be said.

V. Forster Collection

Plate 127: A line-up of steam super-power at the south end of Doncaster Shed, in September 1963, with Class A1 locomotives No. 60149 *Amadis* and No. 60114 *W. P. Allen* in the company of four BR Class 9F 2-10-0 engines which were in their usual filthy state. Main line diesel locomotives were already stabling at this depot in ever-increasing numbers, and although most of these steam engines were withdrawn in the following six months, 36A remained a steam stronghold for a further 2½ years, and had the distinction of being the last operational steam depot on the Eastern Region of BR.

P. Tatlow

Plates 128 & 129:   Dundee (Tay Bridge) in June 1933, with Class D31 No. 9728 seen coming off shed. Thirty years later the NBR-built shed had altered little, except for the addition of new smoke vents, but the motive power had changed considerably with Pacifics in residence along with other Standard LNER types, including Class B1s and V2s. By September 1965, when the lower photograph was taken, there were no more than thirty engines allocated to this Tayside depot and of those, only ten were former NBR locomotives; a far cry from the eighty plus of 1933.

Author's Collection & W. T. Stubbs

Plate 130: The west end of Dunfermline Shed Yard, in the late summer of 1926, with the depot's newly-acquired Darlington-built Class J38s Nos. 1406 and 1410 boosting the goods engine allocation. In the background can be seen the timber-built coaling stage.

National Railway Museum/Stephen Collection

Plate 131: A Sunday morning view of Dunfermline Shed in 1926, with an assortment of pre-grouping locomotives rubbing shoulders with LNER-built engines.

National Railway Museum/Stephen Collection

Plates 132 & 133:   Dunfermline Running Shed, as seen from the coaling stage ramp in the late 1920s. The dark exterior leads one to think that this was a dead-end type shed but, in fact, it was a through shed, with all four roads extending into the east yard. The design is pure NBR, even down to the road numbers above each entrance. The shed remained unaltered until the early BR period, as can be seen in the lower view, taken in April 1952, with a mixture of LNER and BR liveries adorning the engines. Within a few years, though, a new roof had taken the place of the transverse pitches. BR saw fit to expend a large amount of capital on this depot, the original 50ft. turntable being swapped for a 70ft. vacuum unit in 1951, and coal and ash plants being added in 1950. It was little wonder that this should be one of the Scottish Region's last operational steam depots. Closure came on that fateful day in May 1967.

F. Moore & H. C. Casserley

Plate 134: The north end of Eastfield Shed Yard, photographed in the early 1930s. This was a Sunday morning, as can be judged by the large number of the depot's allocation being 'on shed'. During this period of the LNER regime, there were 200 plus engines on the books, and although the shed spanned fourteen roads, there was never enough room to have every engine under cover. Nevertheless the overcrowding made a glorious sight.

Author's Collection

Plate 135: Eastfield, on 29th May 1955, crowded yet again, but this time due to an ASLEF strike which brought together this fine assortment of motive power.

J. F. Henton

Plate 136 (right): Class N15 0-6-2 tank engines, Nos. 9259 and 9452, await their turn to be refuelled at the Eastfield coaling stage in the early 1930s.

T. G. Hepburn

Plate 137 (left): In April 1949, Class A2/2 No. 60505 *Thane Of Fife* stands alongside the remains of Eastfield's manual coaling stage. The Haymarket-based Pacific was shortly to be sent south of the border, to spend the rest of its days at New England.

V. Forster

Plate 138 (right): Eastfield was often the recipient of new LNER-purchased products from the North British Locomotive Co. On 22nd February 1948, brand-new Class B1, No. E1290, pictured in the apple green livery of the LNER but with the name of the new owners on the tender, awaits a running-in turn at the north end of the shed, after delivery from Queens Park Works. It was the practice of Eastfield to run-in all the NBL-built Class B1 engines before they were distributed to various depots, a practice that was carried on during the BR period. This particular locomotive was bound eventually for Stockton.

A. G. Ellis

Plate 139: The apparent conglomeration of engine sheds at East Hartlepool, in August 1936. There were, on this site, 2 three road sheds and a two roader, making a somewhat lengthy and untidy situation. The engines on shed, as can be seen, were an ancient bunch of NER origin. Closure came in April 1939, and the thirty engines still using the depot were reallocated to West Hartlepool.

W. A. Camwell

Plate 140: It was this view of the former NER engine shed at Ferryhill, in 1936, which appeared in a 1951 issue of the *Railways* magazine, and brought to my notice the interest of the engine sheds as well as the locomotives they housed. This shed opened in 1881 to house a dozen or so goods engines although, by the time of the Grouping, twenty odd 0-6-0s of various classes were allocated here, along with two Class G5 0-4-4 tanks that were primarily used for passenger workings. The heyday of the shed came in 1935, when it took on the residue of the Shildon allocation with the closure of that shed. As can be seen in this early August view, most of the engines were still at Ferryhill but just over two years later, Ferryhill itself was closed to steam working although during World War II, some of the exhibits from York Railway Museum were housed there in safe keeping. All trace of the depot and its associated yards has now gone.

W. A. Camwell

Plate 141:   Fort William, standing on the shore of Loch Eil, was opened in 1894 during the NBR's push into the West Highlands, and shared a marvellous isolation with Britain's highest mountain, the nearby Ben Nevis. The two road pitched-roofed shed was built from brick, and apart from the arched windows had a number of attractive architectural features, including six tapered smoke vents, all of which remained unaltered until closure in December 1962. From 1913 onwards the shed housed a number of Reid-designed 4-4-0s (LNER Class D34), built specially for the West Highland line, and during LNER ownership these were supplemented by Class K2 2-6-0s, some of which were named after Scottish lochs. One of these, the last named Class K2 that worked from the shed (No. 61791 *Loch Laggan*), can just be made out, in this September 1959 view, behind Eastfield-allocated Stanier 'Black Five' No. 44996. The other 'Black Five', No. 44973, and Class J36 No. 65300 were local residents, but the Class B1 4-6-0 at the head of the line was yet another Eastfield visitor.

P. Tatlow

Plates 142 & 143 (right): Being a purely freight locomotive depot, Frodingham had its share of WD 2-8-0s in BR days, as well as Class 01, 02 and 04 2-8-0 engines. The upper view of the depot, taken on a weekend in September 1964, shows a large number of its allocation, as well as a couple of Class B1 4-6-0s, coaled up and ready for the week's work ahead. The pre-nationalisation allocation of seventy plus locomotives had dropped to forty odd by the time the Brush diesels arrived in April 1965 (lower photograph) and only ten months later steam was banished altogether, although the depot is still used as a service and stabling point.

W. T. Stubbs

Plate 144: Class A3 Pacific No. 60036 *Colombo* queues up with Class A8 4-6-2 tank No. 69871 for water at Gateshead, in late August 1954. The water crane is one of the LNER standard types that replaced many fine pre-grouping examples, and could be found at almost all the LNER engine sheds. Behind the Class A3 can be seen part of the old Chaytors Bank roundhouse, latterly used as a paint shop for the nearby works.

B. Morrison

Plate 145: Booster-fitted Class C9 Atlantic No. 727 rests on one of the stabling roads at Gateshead in April 1934. The Gateshead complex consisted of four in-line roundhouses running roughly from east to west (numbered 1-4), with a three road straight shed alongside the most westerly shed. This view shows but a small section of No. 2 shed, with one of the access roads in the foreground coming in from the yard which was at the left, out of picture.

H. C. Casserley

Plate 146:   The 'Pacific Shed' at Gateshead in June 1964, looking west. This shed was so-called because Pacific engines could not use any of the depot's roundhouses, due to the internal turntables being, at maximum, only 60ft. in diameter. A 70ft. turntable was installed in No. 1 shed towards the end of steam but for the greater part of their association with the Tyneside depot, the 4-6-2 thoroughbreds were stabled and maintained in this three road establishment. To the left of the shed, behind the Class K1 2-6-0, can be seen the doors of the breakdown crane shed.

W. T. Stubbs

Plate 147:   Eviction at Gateshead, 1964 style. These remnants of the Gateshead steam allocation are gathered around one of the remaining 60ft. turntables still to be found here during that year. Behind is the newly-constructed diesel depot, fashioned from two of the four large square roundhouses that once served the LNER allocation. Still evident is the soot-stained stonework of the original shed that covered this turntable. At this time, Gateshead was the only shed in the country with Class J72 0-6-0 and Class V1 2-6-2 tanks on its books although not for long, as the Class V1s Nos. 67620 and 67628 were soon to be scrapped. Meanwhile the tiny Class J72, No. 69005, which was, in fact, the youngest engine in the picture at a mere fifteen years old, was to become part of the departmental stock. Class B1 4-6-0 No. 61238 *Leslie Runciman* was about to depart south to Ardsley for a new lease of life, hence the lack of a 52A shedplate. These, at this time, were being fitted two at a time to the depot's growing diesel locomotive fleet.

A. George

Plate 148:   The vast width of the former Manchester, Sheffield & Lincolnshire Railway engine shed at Gorton, is clearly visible in this July 1937 view. Opened in 1879, the 'northlight' shed became the largest on the GCR system with twenty stabling roads, and upwards of 200 engines were allocated here by the Grouping. The shed was originally divided between passenger and goods engine types, with a turntable sited on either side of the yard, but with only a single coal stage to serve the huge allocation. Just before the turn of the century, a four road paint shop, belonging to the nearby works, was built on to the west wall of the shed and this can be seen on the left of the picture. The turntable on that side was moved to a position adjacent to the other turntable, on the east side of the yard, while a new double-sided coaling stage was also built at this time, virtually between the two turning units. In the 1930s, further modernisation saw one of the turntables and the coaling stage swept away, when the yard and its associated serving facilities were remodelled.

W. A. Camwell

Plate 149:   Gorton Shed Yard with its ever-present smoke haze, photographed just before the Grouping.
W. A. Brown Collection

Plate 150: Looking to the south-east across Gorton Shed Yard, shortly after the LNER had come into being. Most of the engines on view still carry their former owner's livery. In the centre background can be seen the roof of the coaling stage and to its left the coal pulverisation plant. Gorton Works erecting shop is visible on the right.

W. A. Brown Collection

Plate 151: Class A3 No. 60054 *Prince of Wales*, of 38C Leicester (Central), is seen beside the wet ash pit at Gorton Shed in May 1953, after having worked a 'down' GCR route express into Manchester. The ash pit was one of the largest on the LNER, at a length of 280ft., and was laid down in 1932 as part of the modernisation scheme carried out at Gorton in the early 1930s. A 500 ton capacity twin bunker coaling plant, from which the engine has just reversed, stood just to the west of the ash pit, and was also brought into use in 1932. Class A3s were regular visitors to Gorton until the Woodhead electrification was inaugurated in the mid-1950s, but none had been allocated to the depot since October 1944 when seven of the class were replaced by Class V2 locomotives. The majority of Class A3 allocations to this East Manchester Shed had been short-term affairs starting in 1924 when, designated as Class A1, certain members of the class (including No. 60054) were sent new from Doncaster for running-in purposes. They stayed only a few weeks in most cases but, just before World War II, five of the Pacifics arrived, starting a trend that saw fourteen of the class being allocated during the war years. The longest resident of this handsome breed was No. 2558 (60059) which stayed from September 1938 until December 1942.

B. Hilton

Plate 152 (left): The site of the old coaling stage, located in the south-east corner of Gorton Yard, was laid out as a storage site for engines awaiting entry into the adjacent works. The area was also used for storage of withdrawn engines, arriving at Gorton for the last time in order to be cut up in a yard opposite the running shed, across what was Wellington Street (later Widnes Street). This forlorn looking Class L3 tank, No. 69050, has already received its white cross denoting, at least at Gorton, 'cut up', photographed probably for the last time on the storage site in August 1955.

B. Morrison

Plate 153: Class S1 0-8-4T No. 9901 stands next to the 70ft. turntable at Gorton on 12th October 1947. The Mexborough-based locomotive has just received its new LNER number, resulting from the 1946 renumbering scheme. Many engine types not normally associated with Gorton Shed could be found in the yard, either awaiting entry into works or being run-in after overhaul.

C. A. Appleton

Plate 154: Class B17 4-6-0 No. 2834 *Hinchingbrooke*, backs off Gorton Shed, in 1933, ready to work one of the principal GCR line passenger turns. Gorton had acquired this engine brand-new in 1931 and, by 1933 it was one of six 'Sandringham' class engines allocated there. The class was associated with Gorton, from introduction in 1928, until the final one went south in 1946.

G. Coltas

Plate 155:   Gorton Shed during the 1950s, with evidence of rebuilding having taken place during World War II. Roads Nos. 6 and 8 have been terminated outside the shed and their entrances bricked up, the available space allowing new machinery to be put in. During this period the depot was coded 39A and the allocation was still pure LNER vintage but, in 1956, with the closure of the ex-Midland Railway shed at Belle Vue, former LMS types were allocated here for the first time. Two years later the depot was ceded to the London Midland Region and was coded 9H for a short time but, after only a few months, its final shed code of 9G was taken up. Closure came in June 1965, when the locomotive allocation did not include a single former LNER type.

C. A. Appleton

Plate 156:   Both Atlantic and Pacific locomotives can be made out in this view of the old shed at Grantham in 1937. The shed was built in 1855 as a two road building with an adjacent two road carriage shed, but by 1864 the carriage shed had been taken over by the Locomotive Department. The coaling stage, the roof of which can be seen in the left foreground, was built towards the end of the century and replaced a smaller coke stage.

A. G. Ellis

Plate 157: The four road 'northlight' shed at Grantham, opened in 1894 and seen here from the top of the new coaling plant in 1937.

A. G. Ellis

Plate 158: The 'northlight' shed in 1963, just one day before closure. The roof had been rebuilt to a fashion in the 1950s, but even the austere WD 2-8-0 No. 90598 looked smarter. The hydraulic sheerlegs can be seen on the right, with two of the depot's remaining Class 02s standing beneath.

W. T. Stubbs

Plate 159: Haverton Hill was a typical NER brick-built straight road engine shed of open-ended design, opened in 1898 along with the elevated coaling stage. The allocation consisted exclusively of freight types after 1939, but prior to this there had been a couple of Class F8 2-4-2T locomotives to take care of the depot's few passenger turns. In this July 1954, view three of the shed's Class K1 2-6-0 engines can be seen, along with a Class J27 0-6-0. After this date Class B1 4-6-0s and WD 2-8-0s replaced these types, and a further influx of Class Q6 0-8-0s boosted the allocation to 21 at the time of closure in June 1959.

A. R. Goult

Plate 160: On the edge of the Peak District, the MS&LR built this small shed at Hayfield in 1868. The stone-built structure stood near to the terminus of the branch from New Mills, and was a sub-shed of Gorton. In May 1957, Class C14 4-4-2T No. 67443 was waiting to take the return train to Manchester, the shed by this time having been relegated to overnight stabling only.

A. G. Ellis

Plate 161: Haymarket, pictured in the early 1930s, with Class D29 No. 9245 *Bailie Nicol Jarvie* of Stirling on No. 1 road and one of the depot's own Class A3 Pacifics, No. 2797 *Cicero*, being prepared to work a London bound express. The eight road shed was of typical NBR design, and was responsible for the bulk of the long-distance passenger workings from the Scottish capital.

F. Moore

Plate 162 (left): The cluttered eastern end of Haymarket Depot during the 1950s, with Class B1 4-6-0 No. 61007 *Klipspringer* adding to the general untidyness of the place, with its connecting rods stripped down for maintenance.

Author's Collection

Plate 163: No. 2001 *Cock o' the North* is made ready at Haymarket, to haul the 'Aberdonian' from Waverley on the last leg of its northbound run.

B. Hilton Collection

Plate 164 (right): Not all locomotives allocated to Haymarket were named, and Class J39 No. 64861, in its new BR livery, was one such engine that had Edinburgh shed as its home.

B. Hilton

Plate 165: Haymarket, on 4th July 1954, featuring the usual line-up of Gresley products.

V. Forster Collection

Plate 166: In 1946, the LNER bought a large number of the 'Austerity' 0-6-0 saddle tanks from the Ministry of Supply and here, pictured with its BR number, is No. 68014 acting as 'stage pilot' at Heaton Junction, being the sole representative of its class allocated to this former NER shed. In the background can be seen much activity, as the coaling gang go about topping up the tender of Class A1 Pacific No. 60146 *Peregrine*. The single-sided coaling stage was equipped with three discharge chutes and six water cranes, for servicing the depot's ninety odd engines.

B. Morrison

Plate 167:   This industrial, although picturesque, scene formed the backdrop of Heaton Mersey (CLC) Shed when viewed from the west. The eight road shed was opened in 1889 and its facilities and accommodation was shared by the GNR, MR and MS&LR, although the latter two companies predominated in the number of locomotives stabled here. During the LNER period, former GCR engines formed the larger part of the LNER allocation with, on the eve of nationalisation, thirty odd engines sharing the shed with an equal number of LMS engines. This view of Heaton Mersey, on 8th July 1967 shows, on the left, the part roofless coaling stage, whilst in the yard, BR Standard Class 9Fs and ex-LMS Class 8Fs have taken the place of the smaller pre-grouping designs that were so abundant in the 1950s. The shed closed in May 1968, its few remaining duties being taken over by a new diesel depot which can just be made out behind the top right-hand corner of the coal stage. The new depot remained operational for only a short period as it too, like the steam shed, was demolished. A motorway now cuts through the site, giving no idea of the great railway presence that once graced the area.

D. F. Tee

Plate 168:   Hitchin Shed was sited adjacent to the 'up' platform of the GNR station and this view of the yard, in October 1937, reflects a strong GNR presence amongst the engines on shed. Locomotive facilities were set up here in 1850 and continued for 111 years, until the advent of diesels brought about the shed's closure in June 1961.

W. A. Camwell

Plate 169: Class N1 and N2 0-6-2 tanks galore could be seen at Hornsey on most days, in fact, the first Class N1s arrived here in 1907, just eight years after the shed was opened, with the type being allocated to 34B, as the shed was coded by BR, virtually up to closure in 1961. Holding centre stage, in October 1954, is one of the condensing examples of Class N1 which were used on the Metropolitan Railway's widened lines.

B. Morrison

Plate 170: The former H&BR running shed at Hull (Alexandra Dock) was demolished in 1927 after the shed was virtually ready to fall down. Despite this, engines continued to stable on the site of the two road timber building until the end of steam workings in the area of the docks, and even after that, diesel shunters could be found here stabled overnight. In the later LNER period the usual classes of locomotive found here were J72, J74 and J77 0-6-0Ts, the H&B engines being ousted just after the Grouping by ex-NER types. This mid-1950s view shows the usual weekend gathering, while the allocation in February 1949 was Class J72 Nos. 68670, 68686, 68747, 68748, 68751, 68752 and 68753, Class J73 Nos. 68360 and 68361 and Class J77 Nos. 68401, 68402, 68413, 68429, 68435 and 68440.

B. Hilton Collection

Plate 171: Hull (Springhead) played host to a number of huge Class A7 4-6-2 tank engines during the latter part of the LNER and early BR period. In this view No. 69778, with little more than seven months of its working life left, was photographed at the west end of the former Hull & Barnsley Railway's main shed in October 1954. The eight road shed itself, had only four years left before it was closed after 73 years of use.

B. K. B. Green

Plate 172: Built at the turn of the century, to accommodate the increasing requirement for suburban motive power, the three road 'westernlight' shed at Ilford was sited on the north side of the station. No turntable was laid, as the adjacent triangle formed by the Hainault line sufficed. A small coaling stage, just out of picture to the left, was supplied to refuel the dozen or so tank engines and up to six goods tender engines. This pre-war view of the shed shows the usual types of locomotives allocated. A sub-shed of Stratford, the depot fell victim to the GER lines electrification and was closed by 1939.

W. A. Camwell

Plate 173: Immingham was the last of the GCR's 'large' sheds to be brought into use. Opened in 1912, to coincide with the inauguration of the adjacent extensive dock estate, the twelve road through shed was built with the traditional brick walls, although the foundations and engine pits saw large-scale use of reinforced concrete. The roof over the running shed had transverse pitches, whilst the two road fitting shop, built along the north wall of the shed, had a high single-pitched roof to accommodate lifting machinery. This 1927 view shows the establishment in its original form although the water softener and concrete storage tank, seen on the left, were fairly recent additions. The engines on shed reflected the pure GCR allocation of this period.

Author's Collection

Plate 174 (left): The south end of Immingham in 1947. Prominent behind the sheerlegs is the huge concrete water tank perched on stilts above the coaling stage. The structure remains standing alongside today's modern diesel depot.

J. A. Sommerfield Collection

Plate 175: By 1960, Immingham's running shed roof consisted of this corrugated asbestos affair, supported by a lightweight steel framework, the remains of the original roof having been taken down by BR. The allocation in this year consisted mainly of ex-LNER and BR Standard classes, the few remaining ex-GCR veterans being represented by Class J11 and 04 locomotives. Coded 40B throughout its BR existence, Immingham was closed to steam in 1966 and, to accommodate the vast diesel locomotive fleet that served this thriving district, a large new purpose-built repair and maintenance shed was erected. The steam shed was subsequently torn down, although sections of the old fitting shop have survived and are used to this day.

W.T. Stubbs

Plates 176 & 177: The LNER had planned, in 1938, to modernise the former GER engine establishment at Ipswich (Halifax Junction) at a total cost of £76,000. The whole depot was in urgent need of renewal and the staff, who had to look after more than 100 locomotives of varying age and origin, in what were then described as cramped, ancient and atrocious conditions, must have breathed a sigh of relief at the news. Just one year later, though, before any serious reconstruction could begin, World War II intervened and so the ambitious project was curtailed, leaving the artisans of Ipswich to struggle on until the early 1950s when BR finally rebuilt the shed and its facilities. These two views, taken in August 1956, show the modernised depot as seen from the main line (upper), and the rear yard looking south, with the coaling plant on the left.

British Rail

Plate 178:   A tidy yard at Keith (ex-GNSR) Locomotive Shed in the 1930s, with Class D41 4-4-0s Nos. 6882, 6905 and 6907 sharing the scene with Class B12 4-6-0 No. 8501. The latter was one of a number of the B12 class sent to the Great North of Scotland Section in 1931, some of them spending the next twenty years there. The group of men alongside No. 6907 are obviously enthusiasts exchanging notes and are probably far from home, as travelling cases of various sizes can be seen in front of the pile of rail chairs. Can any reader recognise anyone?

F. Moore

Plate 179:   The approach to King's Cross Station was probably the most photographed of all the London termini, and on the right of this June 1931 view the station locomotive yard, with a number of Class N2 tank engines resting between duties can be seen. A solitary Atlantic, No. 4458, and a Pacific are also discernible. The engine yard was established on this site in 1923, after station enlargements had forced the move from a previous site nearer to the suburban platforms. Facilities included a 70ft. turntable, manually-operated at first but later fitted with a vacuum tractor, and a small coaling plant as well as adequate stabling lines. This small servicing area enabled light engine movements to and from 'Top Shed' to be kept to a minimum, and so, to a great extent, relieved the main line tunnels. The first locomotive facilities were set up at the station in 1862, when heavy traffic was already causing congestion through the tunnels, but enlargement of the station caused these facilities to be resited on a number of occasions. This, the final position of the yard, was used until the days of the 'Deltics'.

BR/OPC Collection

Plate 180 (left): A typical early morning line-up at King's Cross Shed in the 1930s, with tenders full and plenty of steam. This capable looking bunch are ready to work northbound trains and earn the LNER some much-needed revenue.
National Railway Museum

Plate 181: A study of front ends at King's Cross Shed in May 1954. The Classes B1, V2 and A1 are from Thompson, Gresley and Peppercorn respectively.

C. R. L. Coles

Plate 182: Kirkby Stephen, on 24th July 1939, and this Westmorland outpost of the LNER basks in the midday sunshine. On the shed yard can be seen Class E4 2-4-0 No. 7416 and Class J21 0-6-0 No. 981, whilst inside the shed were Class E4 No. 7496, Class G5 0-4-4T No. 1916 and Class J25 0-6-0s Nos. 1979 and 1994. The former NER stone-built shed had its origins in the South Durham & Lancashire Union Railway, when a small shed was erected in 1861 to accommodate two engines, but later extensions and alterations brought the shed up to its present size. To the left of the twin two road sheds can be seen the coaling platform, complete with a hand crane and 1 ton capacity tubs, this platform being replaced in the post-war years by an electric coaling hoist. Beyond the coaling platform was a 50ft. manual turntable. Coded 'KBY STN' in LNER days, the code 51H was applied by BR, but in 1958 the depot became part of the LMR and was given the code 12E. This was appropriate, as the allocation by then consisted of a mainly LMS flavour, with Ivatt 2-6-0s sharing the place with BR Standard 2-6-0s, but by April the code was changed to 12D, its last before closure in November 1961.

C. A. Appleton

Plates 183 & 184: Two contrasting views of the ex-Great North of Scotland Railway semi-roundhouse at Kitty-brewster. The upper view, taken in August 1935 from across the manual type turntable, shows the shed virtually in its original condition, while the lower view, taken some nineteen years later, shows the radical changes which had taken place. The turntable by now was vacuum-operated and the stone arch opening of the shed has gone, although new doors have been fitted to the more conventional openings. The coaling plant in the background has already been described in *Plate 29*.

W. L. Good & Photomatic

Plate 185: Opened just after the turn of the century, Langwith Junction was built to provide motive power for the vast amount of coal traffic originating from the area. Typical of many of the East Midlands engine sheds, the allocation consisted almost exclusively of freight engines, with a handful of tank engines to cover both yard work and any local passenger jobs. This July 1954 scene shows a good cross section of classes of engine to be found here during the BR period, with WD 2-8-0s sharing stabling room with an almost wholly ex-GCR stud. The two road 'northlight' shed, seen here on the left, sufficed until the mid-LNER period when a three road corrugated iron clad pitched roof dead end shed was erected alongside. Closed in February 1966, when a new diesel depot was opened at nearby Shirebrook, 41J, as Langwith was coded in 1958, fell into a state of dereliction and was eventually demolished, although the coal traffic it was built to serve still flourishes.

N. E. Preedy

Plate 186 (left): The south end of the 'northlight' shed at Langwith Junction, on 30th August 1936, with Class N5 tank engine No. 5903 standing alone amongst the ex-GCR tender locomotives.

W. A. Camwell

Plate 187: An interior view of the GCR's Leicester Shed, taken sometime prior to World War I. GCR Class 8B Atlantic No. 192 and Class 11B 4-4-0 No. 1038 both show off the pre-grouping related cleanliness, even down to the burnished buffer heads. Details of the shed's construction can be discerned, as can the prominent slope on the right-hand side of the engine pit floor. To the right of No. 1038 can be seen part of the shed's inside lifting gantry, while outside, of course, was a set of sheerlegs for removing larger items such as driving wheels.

B. Matthews Collection

Plate 188: Situated midway on the line from Northallerton to Hawes, Leyburn Engine Shed was erected for the opening of that line in 1856. The tiny stone-built shed was disused from 1915 until 1939, when a Class G5 0-4-4T was sent there in June of that year. Final closure came in May 1954 when the two resident engines, Class G5 No. 67345 and Sentinel No. 68159, were sent away. Facilities at the shed included a 42ft. 4in. turntable, and coaling was achieved by siting a wagon on an adjacent track and transferring fuel by shovel which, thankfully for the enginemen, was only a once daily occurrence. Behind the shed can be seen two cottages, these being provided for the footplate crew in 1866. This view of Leyburn, in June 1963, shows the shed still very much intact, if a little weed grown.

W. T. Stubbs

Plate 189: This fine panoramic view of the ex-GCR shed at Lincoln, taken in August 1936, shows all the depot's facilities, from the 15 ton capacity Cowans, Sheldon & Co breakdown crane on the left, to the coaling stage on the right. Locomotives are, from the left, Class K2 No. 4673 coming on shed, Class K3 No. 135 and Class K2 No. 4653 under the sheerlegs, Class B5 No. 5185 and Class D2 No. 4376 on No.1 road, Class B4 No. 6096 on No. 2 road and Class B5 No. 6072 on the right. The shed retains its original roof and the ornate arched openings that were so much a part of 19th century shed design. At Lincoln, the GER and GNR also had engine sheds but the GER establishment at Pyewipe Junction was closed shortly after the Grouping, leaving the former GCR and GNR sheds to form a running department under one control, but retaining the two separate sheds.

W. A. Camwell

Plate 190: Loch Leven was, as can be seen, a long narrow single road shed. Originally only half as long as this 1953 photograph depicts, the engine shed was of NBR origin and lasted intact and in use until the early years of BR ownership.

A. G. Ellis

Plate 191:   Mallaig in 1913, with unrebuilt Holmes 0-6-0 No. 751 basking in the sunshine and a stiff breeze blowing off the Sound of Sleat. The stone-built engine shed was erected for the opening of the line to Mallaig from Banavie in 1901, and stood unaltered until closure some 61 years later.

A. C. Roberts

Plate 192:   It was possible, in the days of steam, for shed staff to manoeuvre engines into a good position so that enthusiasts could photograph them. Thus, in this June 1937 shot of Mallaig, it seems that the staff are obliging a group of photographers by turning the 108 ton bulk of Class K2/2 No. 4692 *Loch Eil* and tender around the 52ft. diameter turntable. The scene is little changed from the previous picture except for the engines and some additional huts, one a grounded carriage body acting as the depot general office.

H. C. Casserley

Plate 193: Sporting its 31B (March) shed plate, Class V2 No. 60830 stands at the north end of the wash-out shed at its home depot in July 1961. These superb locomotives were regular visitors to March for many years, but it was not until the late 1950s that any of the class were allocated here. Even then they enjoyed only a short sojourn, as the depot closed to steam locomotives in 1963.

A. G. Ellis

Plate 194: Nearly three years after being absorbed into the LNER, the former Midland & Great Northern Railway shed at Melton Constable shows off a distinctly LNER stud in August 1939, with only a few M&GN examples on shed.

W. A. Camwell

Plate 195: A busy scene at Mexborough in July 1961, with the full width of the shed forming the background for Robinson, Riddles and even Stanier products which grace the yard. Just out of picture to the right was the 60ft. turntable, whilst beyond that was the coaling stage. The water tower, with its adjacent water softening plant, can be seen in the background.

W. T. Stubbs

Plate 196: Lined up military fashion, and looking fairly clean, are these Class 04 2-8-0s at Mexborough, in the summer of 1955. At the time this ex-GCR shed had little more than a dozen Class 04s allocated to it, so most were probably in this picture. Of the 100 plus locomotives shedded at Mexborough in this period, fifty odd were WD 2-8-0s with a dozen Class 02s and the same number of Class J11 0-6-0s. Passenger and mixed traffic types were represented by Class B1s and K3s, whilst the tank engine population contained nothing larger than a few Class N5 0-6-2s, the massive Class S1 0-8-4 tanks having departed to Doncaster eighteen months previously after a long residence lasting nearly fifty years.

B. Hilton Collection

Plate 197: One of the dilapidated ex-NER roundhouses at Middlesbrough, in May 1954, with a party of 'shed bashers' noting the numbers of the Class Q6 0-8-0 locomotives stabled outside. There were three similar round-house sheds at this place, all grouped together and built at different periods from 1866 to 1872, although there had been an engine shed at Middlesborough prior to 1845, the site of which was later used for station extensions. Coded 51D in BR days, the depot was closed at the end of May 1958, and its engines and men were transferred to the newly-built and spacious motive power depot at nearby Thornaby.

Photomatic

Plate 198: Middleton-in-Teesdale, pictured in September 1956, was yet another example of the small, end of the branch, engine shed with a slated pitched roof on stone walls and an arched opening. The shed was ready for use in early 1870 and reputedly cost £196 to build, although this did not include the 45ft. turntable which was installed at a later date. Throughout its life the tiny depot housed a wide variety of locomotives under its roof, especially during LNER days. Tender engines predominated on the branch although just before World War II, tank engines became regular residents. The shed closed in September 1957, and was demolished four years later.

R. M. Tomkins

*Plate 199:*Montrose (ex-NBR) in June 1957, with no motive power on shed. The timber clad shed was, by this time, in a run-down state and in need of a coating of creosote. A coaling stage stood just out of picture to the left, although it was disused during much of the BR period with most refuelling being carried out from an open wagon on one of the shed roads until closure of the shed in late 1966. The grounded six wheel coach acted as the office/messroom. Access to the shed for locomotives was via the turntable, as can be seen in the picture.

A. G. Ellis

Plate 200: Neasden (GCR), with a brand-new Class 11E 4-4-0 standing alongside a small snowplough in April 1914. The shed was a mere fifteen years old and was the last of the Extension sheds to open, closure came in 1962 after four years of LMS control.

L&GRP Courtesy David & Charles

Plates 201 & 202:   The first engine shed at New England was a small affair opened by the GNR in 1851. Over the next fifteen years expansion of the site saw a number of large sheds and a locomotive repair works spring up, making it one of the largest depots on the GNR. The New England site was surrounded by a large triangle, so the need for turntables never arose. By the turn of the century there were nearly 200 engines allocated here, but this number was exceeded for most of the LNER and early BR periods, reflecting the shed's importance. The upper view, taken before the Grouping, shows the south end of the through shed with, on the right, the locomotive repair shops. In the lower photograph, taken in September 1963, the large water softener and the coaling plant, both erected during the LNER period, are evident and tower above the engine sheds. This evening view of the place seems appropriate, with long shadows being cast over a yard full of dirty engines, some of them former East Coast Main Line 'Sprinters' which have been relegated to mundane parcels and freight trains. The shed, having been rebuilt during the previous decade, had less than eighteen months operational service left before closure, and the atmosphere of pervading gloom seems evident.

Author's Collection & M. S. Houlgrave

A SELECTION OF THE LARGER NEW ENGLAND RESIDENTS AND VISITORS

Plate 203 (left): Class A3 No. 4475 *Flying Fox*, pictured alongside the coaling stage in June 1935.

L. Hanson

Plate 204 (right): Class A4 No. 4903 *Peregrine*, pictured in its original form during the latter part of 1938.

V. Forster Collection

Plate 205 (left): Yet another Gresley streamlined locomotive, the sole Class W1 4-6-4 No. 10000, fashioned from the 'Hush-Hush'.

V. Forster Collection

Plate 206 (left): Raven Pacific No. 2401 *City of Kingston upon Hull*, looking somewhat outdated next to its recently-acquired eight wheel tender, seen at New England in June 1935.

L. Hanson

Plate 207 (right): Class V2 No. 60881 in February 1962, complete with double chimney and outside steam pipes. New England Shed could boast an allocation of more than thirty of these useful engines, from their introduction until final withdrawal.

V. Forster Collection

Plate 208 (left): The final form of big engines to grace the yards at New England, was the magnificent BR Standard Class 9F 2-10-0s. Here No. 92146 carries New England's last shed code, 34E, in May 1963.

V. Forster Collection

Plate 209 (left): The enginemens' lobby at New England, as it was during BR days. Every locomotive crew came through here, whether starting or finishing a shift, and shed permits were often presented at either of the two windows by visitors.

British Rail

Plate 210 (right): A typical messroom, albeit a little tidier than most. This is New England in 1957.

British Rail

Plate 211 (left): An external view of New England's messroom and general office. In relation to the size of the depot here, the facilities afforded to the enginemen were scant.

British Rail

Plate 212:   An elevated view of the former GCR shed at New Holland, photographed in July 1938, with Class J10 No. 5684 backing out of the shed, whilst inside on this day were Class D3s Nos. 4303 and 4316, Class B5 No. 5181 and tiny Class Y3 No. 21. The roof of the shed is of interest, with its curved barn-like profile of LNER origin. The original roof consisted of two pitched sections, while the four doorways into the shed were, at one time, all arched, very similar to the GCR's Lincoln Shed. New Holland was a sub-shed of Immingham and was officially closed for locomotive purposes in April 1941 but, like many such occurrences, the shed was used many times for stabling engines, well into BR days.

W. A. Camwell

Plate 213:   Situated next to the Stockton line at Northallerton, the engine shed could easily be missed by anyone travelling along the East Coast Main Line through the station seen in the left background. This view of the north end of the shed, in May 1937, leads one to believe that the shed was comprised of only one road when, in fact, it was a two road affair, access to the longer section of the building being gained from the south. The shed's only Class J21 0-6-0, No. 1513, stands out in the rain, whilst inside were Class G5 No. 439, Class J26 No. 442, Class J27 No. 1047 and Class J77 No. 604.

W. A. Camwell

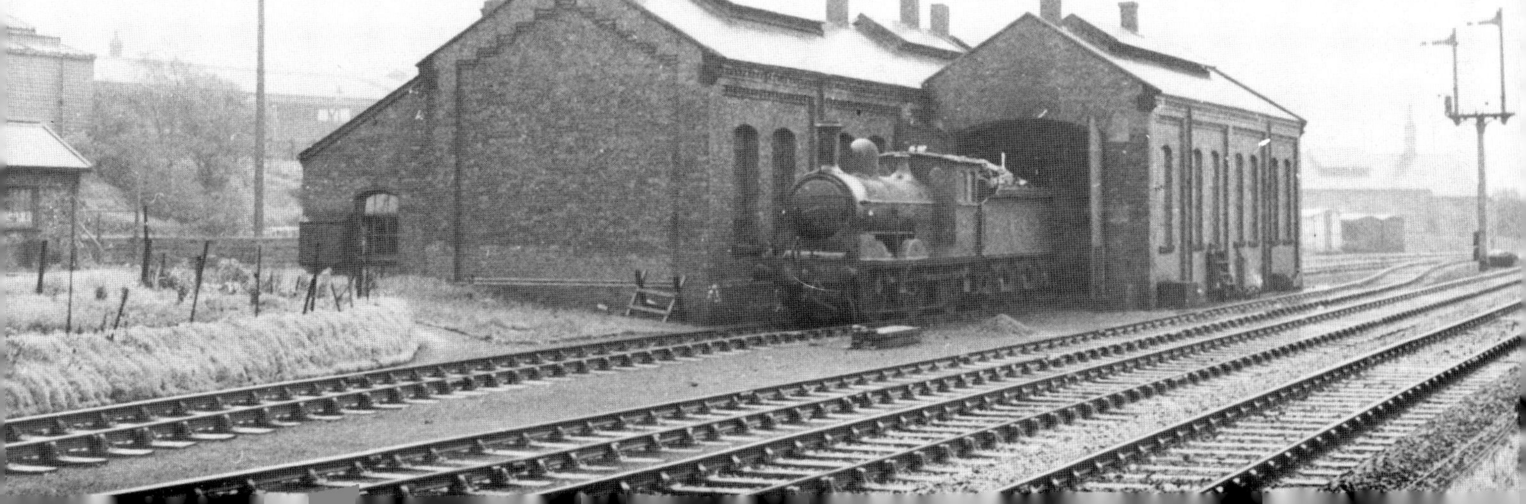

Plate 214: Standing at the end of the branch from Drem, North Berwick's terminal facilities included this superb hipped-roofed engine shed of NBR origin. In this view, taken on 9th July 1952, the unusually high smoke exhausts are worthy of note. Class C15 and C16 tanks, supplied by St. Margaret's, were the usual motive power found at this shed.

A. G. Ellis

Plate 215: Northwich (CLC) Shed, pictured from the station footbridge in June 1952, with Class J10 0-6-0 No. 65131 at the head of a somewhat ancient rake of vehicles forming the breakdown train. The four road engine shed had, by this time, been rebuilt with a 'louvre' type concrete roof and the allocation was strongly in favour of the LMS, with Class 8F 2-8-0 locomotives forming the bulk of the resident engines alongside the few remaining ex-GCR types. Northwich Shed survives today as a diesel servicing and fuelling establishment although gone, of course, are the sheerlegs and the coal shed. Steam can still be seen here at certain weekends when preserved locomotives stable at this shed between hauling specials, or when en route to and from the Severn Valley Railway and the National Railway Museum.

D. Clayton

Plates 216 & 217: The M&GN engine shed at Norwich was known as 'City', and this view of the substantial two road building, with M&GN 4-4-0 No. 53 simmering outside, was taken just prior to LNER ownership. In the early part of World War II, the shed was severely damaged during an enemy bombing raid on the city and in the lower view, taken in July 1958, the austere style of the new shed, supplied by the LNER, is seen shortly before the depot and the railway it served was closed completely.

A. G. Ellis & A. R. Goult

Plate 218: The former GER engine shed at Norwich (Thorpe) in 1933, with two of the shed's principal express passenger engines on the yard, Class B12 4-6-0s Nos. 8523 and 8569, both with ACFI apparatus. Class J17 goods engine No. 8213, being of a lesser breed, has obviously not had the same attention from the cleaners as its bigger brothers. Just visible on the right is part of the depot's coaling stage.

F. Moore

Plate 219: A distant view of Norwich (Thorpe) in the late 1950s, with some of the depot's 'Britannia' class Pacifics on shed. By this time the shed roof had been rebuilt, a 250 ton capacity coaling plant had been erected along with a water softening plant, and a 70ft. turntable had been laid. Gone were the Class B12s, but still going about their daily duties were the Class J17s with No. 65519, seen in the foreground, representing the ten members of its class still allocated to 32A.

D. J. Montgomery

Plate 220: Nottingham (Arkwright Street), on 14th July 1935, with Doncaster-based Class K3 No. 1141 gracing the yard. The former GCR shed was opened in 1898, in readiness for the opening of the London Extension, and was of standard period construction with 'northlight' roof and a centrally-placed clock over the stabling roads. Inside the shed on this day were Class D3 4-4-0s No. 3400 and 4309 (both of Colwick), Nos. 4319 and 4352, Class D9 4-4-0 No. 6032, Class J11 0-6-0s Nos. 5235 (of Annesley), Nos. 5993 and 6078.

W. A. Camwell

Plate 221: Glasgow (Parkhead), on 19th April 1947, and Class J37 0-6-0 No. 4563, one of the shed's residents, gets ready to move off to the nearby sidings for a days work. The recently ex-works engine is already showing off a good smattering of coal dust, with at least a shovelful on the cab roof.

A. G. Ellis

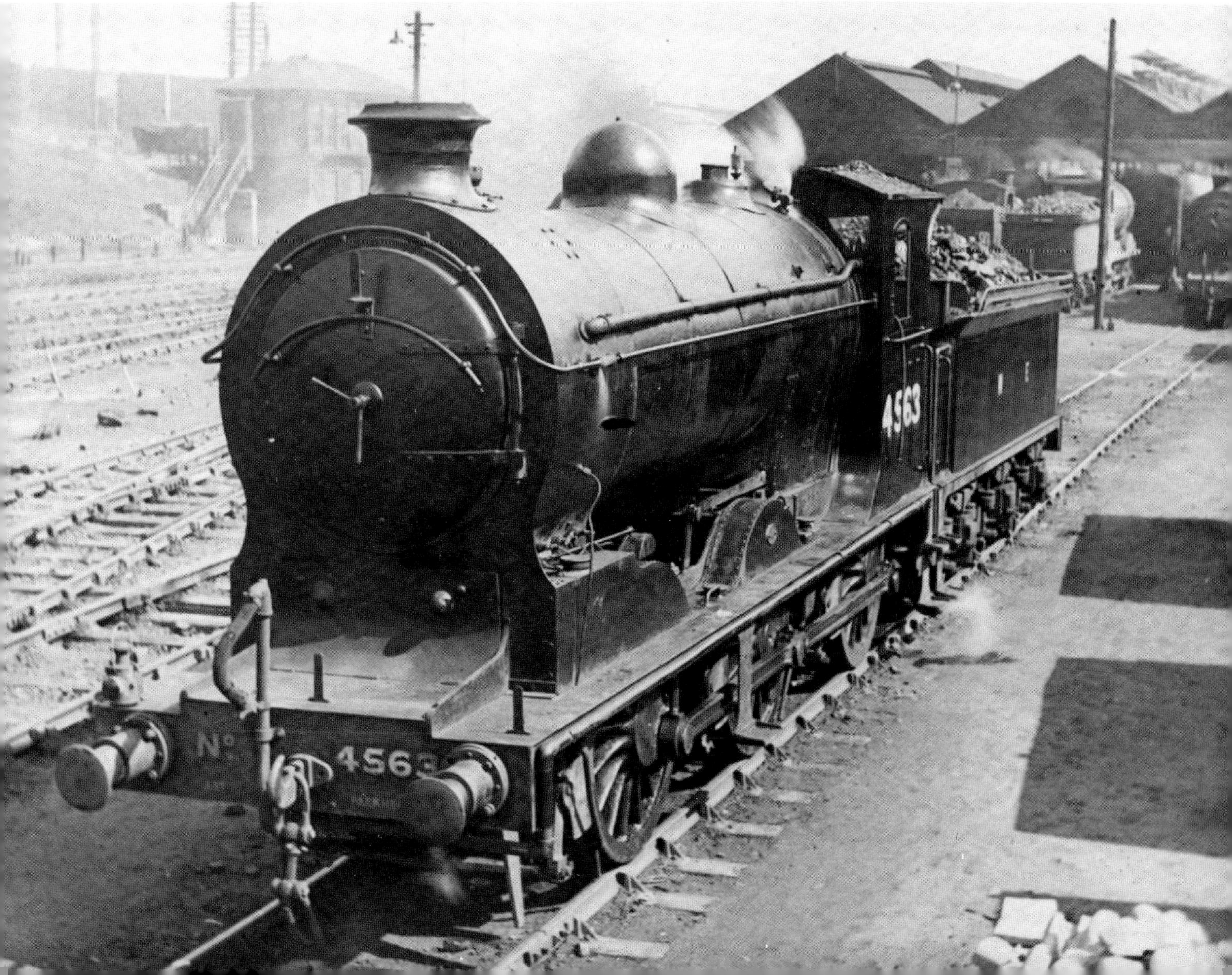

Plate 222:   In March 1937, that intrepid photographer *'Cam'* was busy climbing again in order to get a better vantage point, this time to capture the ex-GER shed and its yard at Parkeston Quay. Some 22 engines were on shed, and prominent on the right, in apple green livery, is Class B17 4-6-0 No. 2836 *Harlaxton Manor*.

W. A. Camwell

Plate 223:   The timber-built engine shed at Pateley Bridge, in July 1935, with Class G5 No. 1912 just visible in the shadows of the interior. An engine shed had been erected here as early as 1862 when the branch up the Nidd Valley was completed, but this building lasted as home for the branch engine until 1951.

W. A. Camwell

Plate 224: A small servicing facility was available for locomotives at Penistone where the MS&LR had provided sidings, a coaling shelter and a turntable. Here we see Class N4 No. 5718 and Class N5 No. 5545 resting between duties alongside the shelter in the late 1930s.

W. A. Camwell

Plate 225: Perth (NBR) in the 1930s, with Class D30 No. 9417 *Cuddie Headrigg* having smokebox debris cleaned out, whilst alongside is the smaller Class D31 No. 9574. Both were Perth-based engines, and their cleanliness reminds one of the ease with which the railway companies could keep locomotives clean, using the abundant cheap labour of the time.

A. A. Maclean Collection

Plate 226: Polmont was opened by the NBR in 1914 to replace a small shed at Bo'ness Junction. The building was of period design, but timber cladding was used for the walls instead of the customary brick construction. Surprisingly the shed withstood the rigours of time and smoke pollution, and closed, virtually unaltered, in 1964. This view, looking west in 1932, shows the typical 0-6-0 locomotives which were predominant in the allocation list, while the surrounding landscape, with its slag heaps, gives an idea of the shed's traffic with coal being the main produce of the area. The allocation hovered around the forty plus mark for much of the depot's lifespan, and there was nearly always a named Class J36 on the books. The manual coaling stage and 51ft. 6in. diameter turntable sufficed, and modernisation of any sort hardly ever touched the place, and even the engines found on shed in later years were mostly pre-grouping types, with just a handful of Gresley products and occasional BR Standards.

Author's Collection

Plate 227: Polmont in June 1936, this time looking north.　　*W. A. Camwell*

Plate 228:   The former NBR engine shed at Reedsmouth became part of the North Eastern Area of the LNER shortly after the Grouping, an appropriate move on the part' of the authorities as the shed was located in the county of Northumberland. The allocation during the LNER and BR period comprised, in the main, ex-NER locomotives, the last two engines allocated at closure in September 1952 being Class J21s Nos. 65033 and 65119. A visit in the 1970s found the shed still intact, but being used by a farmer as a home for his livestock. This photograph was taken in the July of the shed's last year of operation.

A. G. Ellis

Plate 229:   Riccarton Junction Engine Shed was, as can be seen, a lean-to structure built on to the coaling stage, with a 55ft. turntable completing the facilities. Class J36 0-6-0 No. 65316 of St. Margaret's Depot has a tender cab, an item that was so necessary when working the bleak Waverley route.

A. G. Ellis

Plates 230 & 231:   Two views of Retford (ex-GCR) Locomotive Depot, showing the overcrowding that occurred on most weekends at this small three road shed. The upper view shows engines being parked up, in July 1960, with Class 02 2-8-0 locomotives predominating and a solitary Class J11 representing the 0-6-0 group. The lower picture shows the view looking west from London Road, in May 1963, and in addition to the mass of 2-8-0s on show, the shed itself can be seen in the left background. BR had rebuilt the shed in the early 1950s and had used, surprisingly, a 'northlight' style roof to replace the previous dilapidated single pitch effort. The three engines on the extreme right of the yard were withdrawn by this time, and were awaiting dispatch to Gorton to be cut up. In fact, within two years of the lower photograph being taken, most of the engines on view had dropped their fires for the last time. The sheerlegs, it will be noted, have also been taken out of commission, and this was yet another sign of falling maintenance standards for the steam locomotive.

K. C. H. Fairey & J. A. Sommerfield

Plate 232: A pre-grouping scene, at St. Margaret's, with some vintage NBR steam on show.

A. G. Ellis

Plate 233: The old North Eastern Railway shed at St. Margaret's, pictured in the mid-1930s, with typical Sunday overcrowding in evidence. During this period, as indeed for most of its existence, St. Margaret's had an allocation of 200 plus locomotives, and even when its half dozen sub-sheds are taken into account, there was never enough room to stable all the engines under cover, so scenes like this were regular. The square roundouse was built by the NBR for NER use in 1870, but was taken over fully by the NBR in 1902 and became just one of a number of NBR engine sheds built either side of the main line in this Edinburgh district. All the identifiable engines in the picture are St. Margaret's-based, as are the three large grounded snowploughs in summer storage.

W. E. Boyd

Plate 234: The original NBR roundhouse at St. Margaret's had no roof cladding in 1937, and hitherto unobtainable views could be captured under the shadows of the exposed joists. This attractive scene reveals four of the depot's dozen Class Y9 0-4-0 saddle tanks gathered around the 42ft. diameter turntable in June of that year.

H. C. Casserley

Plate 235: No. 9661 *Ole Bill*, NBR style. This Class J36 locomotive stands just across the main line from the 1846 roundhouse at St. Margaret's in the late 1920s. For the 'spotter', hunting down former NBR locomotives, St. Margaret's was probably the perfect shed for both quantity and variety.

Author's Collection

Plate 236: A general view of St. Margaret's straight shed and the yard, during the early BR period of ownership.

C. Sanderson

Plate 237: Engines big and small at St. Margaret's, on a dull June day in 1961. Neither of the two Pacifics on view was allocated to 64A at this time as, in fact, only three Class A3s were on the books, having arrived in 1960, the first Pacifics to be allocated since 1940. Just prior to the closure of Haymarket, a large influx of Class A1, A2, A3 and A4 locomotives were housed at St. Margaret's to work out their remaining lives, and no less than 24 of the East Coast Main Line 'glamour' engines ended their days there.

W. T. Stubbs

Plate 238: After withdrawal from operating stock in October 1962, Class N15/2 0-6-2T No. 69128 became one of the St. Margaret's Depot stationery boilers, joining the permanent boiler on the site of the old roundhouse. Photographed in 1964, whilst still engaged on this degrading duty, the North British Locomotive Company-built engine has lost some of its detailed fittings, but is virtually intact. The untidy mess around the site was typical of the period when the authorities turned a blind eye on the steam depots and everything to do with steam, wanting only to be rid of what they considered a nuisance as soon as possible. In this case, they didn't have long to wait.

A. George

Plate 239: One of the smaller, and therefore more photographic, NER roundhouses was this unit at Scarborough. The shed was not a standard square roundhouse in size, although the building style was 'period' with a 44ft. 8in. diameter turntable, set down inside and off centre to enable at least some of the stabling roads to be capable of accommodating an engine. Because of its limited space, an eight road straight shed was erected, some eight years later, slightly to the south. One wonders how many heads rolled for allowing such a building to be erected in the limited area available at the time. The shed, in fact, was little used after 1890 except for storage and some repairs of engines. Outside, a 50ft. turntable was laid down, a view of which is shown in *Plate 58.*

J. A. Sommerfield Collection

Plate 240: The straight shed at Scarborough in August 1961, by which time the four roads nearest to the main line had no cover. That part of the shed was taken down in the 1950s, because ground subsidence had rendered the walls unsafe. The roundhouse, featured in the previous photograph, was sited out of picture to the left. The allocation here rarely exceeded more than thirty, but in the summer months, excursions brought in motive power which would stretch the depot's facilities and stabling room to the limit. Closed to steam at the start of the summer timetable in 1963, the depot's facilities continued to be used by visiting steam locomotives until their demise from the North Eastern Region a few years later.

W. T. Stubbs

Plate 241: The roundhouses of the NER were difficult to photograph externally, but inside some superb views were caught by patient cameramen. This view, taken inside one of the Selby roundhouses on 28th August 1932, has found five home-based engines gathered around the covered turntable. From left to right are Class D22 No. 673, Class D17 No. 1637, Class J71 No. 972 and Class N8s Nos. 445 and 861.

H. C. Casserley

Plate 242: In late October 1938, Class B15 4-6-0 No. 817 of York has just left the coaling plant, and is about to proceed into the nearest roundhouse at Selby for turning. Even in the gloomy weather, the vast expanse of the two adjacent square roundhouses is easily seen.

C. A. Appleton

Plate 243: An interesting aerial view of Southport (CLC) Terminus from the north, sometime in the late 1940s. The occasion was probably the annual Southport Flower Show which always brought plenty of traffic, both rail and road, to this north-west resort, hence the reason why stabling room was at a premium both at the goods yard and the running shed in the centre of the picture. The two road brick-built shed, along with the turntable and coaling platform, was brought into use in 1884 and closed in 1952.

Author's Collection

Plate 244:   A close up view of Southport in July 1929, with Class D7 No. 5852 on the turntable.

Dr J. R. Hollick per R. A. Griffiths

Plate 245: Starbeck was one of the longest two road engine sheds in the British Isles, its origins going back to 1857 when the NER opened the first section of the shed. This was just under 100ft. in length, but numerous extensions during the 19th century finally brought the shed up to its long through type layout by 1901. Prior to nationalisation, the depot could boast an allocation of fifty or more locomotives, nearly two thirds of them being tank engines ranging in size from the tiny Class Y3 'Sentinel' up to Pacific tanks of Classes A7 and A8. North Eastern Railway 4-4-0s were always on the books for the long-distance passenger workings from Harrogate and, in this May 1951 view of the north end of the shed, we see Class D49 No. 62773 *The South Durham*, just one of more than a dozen Class D49 engines allocated here at this time.

A. R. Goult

Plate 246: Class J10 No. 5814 stands cold and silent in the somewhat unusually sunlit and smoke-free interior of Staveley Running Shed in 1931. The underside details of the 'northlight' roof are well depicted.

G. Coltas

Plate 247: The cleanliness of Class N4 No. 5720 (later 69245) shows off its handsome and well-proportioned design outside Staveley Shed in 1931. This engine was built in the same year that the shed here was opened and the class, ex-GCR Class 9A, was associated with the depot during most of its existence, with nearly two dozen allocated here at the Grouping. All types of work was performed by these versatile engines, from local passenger duties to haulage of coal trains and piloting.

G. Coltas

Plate 248: The former MS&LR shed at Staveley, photographed in July 1954, with the number of covered stabling roads cut down from twelve to a mere five. The shed was rebuilt in the early 1950s due to the dangerous state of its dilapidated roof, but the office section still retains its original 'northlight' roof and the ornate bay window overlooking the shed yard. On the right can be seen the lofty brick-built coaling stage, which served the depot until closure in 1965.

W. Potter

Plate 249: An all too common sight at motive power depots, in the 1950s and 60s, were the lines of stored or withdrawn locomotives. The fact that an engine had a covering over its chimney usually meant that it was 'stored awaiting further use' but all too often, this hibernation period was the last one many engines spent on shed. Such was the eagerness of the authorities to scrap certain types, that whole classes would disappear overnight. Here we see Class D11 No. 62669 *Ypres*, with other members of its class at Staveley Shed, awaiting the final call.

Author's Collection

Plate 250: Stockton, on 23rd July 1939, with four of the depot's Class A8 4-6-2 tanks on show. This was to be the last summer that these big tank engines were allocated to the Teesside Shed, as World War II brought a virtual halt to their main work along the North Yorkshire coastline to Scarborough. Stockton Shed was opened in 1891 by the NER, its facilities including a standard coaling stage and a 46ft. turntable to serve the thirty or so engines which were allocated in the early years. By the time of the Grouping, nearly fifty locomotives were on the books. Depression in the 1930s saw the number of engines here drop below twenty, mainly because of the closure of the nearby marshalling yard. By the end of that decade, though, the allocation was back to 1923 levels, due to wartime traffic and the reopening of the Stockton Yards. The usual freight engines shedded here included Classes J21, J26 and J27 0-6-0s as well as Class Q5 0-8-0 locomotives, while tank engine types were too numerous to mention. In the early BR period, Class B1 and B16 locomotives saw use of the depot but by mid-June 1959 closure came, and so ended 68 years of locomotive use of the eight road shed.

C. A. Appleton

Plate 251: The Jubilee Shed at Stratford, as seen just before World War I. This twelve road through shed was built during the mid-1880s, to supplement a six road shed that was sited behind the administration block on the left of the picture. The GER domain at Stratford was both huge and complex and when this shed opened, it enabled the whole of the locomotive running department to be sited in one place. The earlier Eastern Counties and Northern & Eastern sheds, standing some distance away to the south, were handed over to the main works, and both the GER-built sheds served steam until its demise on the GER section of BR.

National Railway Museum

Pte 252: The south end of Stratford's Jubilee Shed, as seen from the coaler in the early 1930s, with the usual mass gathering of ex-GER motive power representing numerous classes. This kind of scene could be found on any Sunday until the late 1950s.

British Rail

Plate 253: Ex-works Class D13 4-4-0, No. 8020 of March and Class F3 2-4-2T No. 8044 of Cambridge, wait at the west end of Stratford Shed Yard, in 1932, for their fires to be relit.

G. Coltas

Plate 254: Tucked away on the west side of the roundhouse at Sunderland (South Dock) was a four road straight shed, and here we see two of the depot's Class G5 tanks, Nos. 67259 and 67297, standing alongside a corner of the shed in the summer of 1956. The shed had been recently rebuilt by BR, from the dilapidated remains of a shed dating from the last century. The roundhouse, a section of which can be seen on the right, dated from the mid-1870s.

D. J. Montgomery

Plate 255: The Elsenham & Thaxted Light Railway was worked from its inauguration by GER locomotives. A small shed, seen here in the 1930s, was erected for the opening of the line in March 1913 to house the branch engines, two 'Jubilee' class 0-6-0 tank engines. The shed, built in brick with a slated pitched roof, had a well bored alongside to provide water, which was pumped into the overhead storage tank. Coaling facilities were basic with, as was usual for these small sheds, a wagon drawn alongside the locomotive stabling road, but at least the wagon road was raised which cut down some of the effort of transferring fuel to the engine's bunker. The line was never a busy one, with agricultural produce and some passenger trains providing the bulk of the traffic. Class J15 0-6-0 engines occasionally worked the branch, but the more usual performers were Class J67, J68 and J69 tank engines. It fell to Class J69 No. 68579 to work the last passenger train in September 1952 and from then on, the shed, a sub-shed to Cambridge, hardly saw a resident engine and was closed, together with the branch, on 1st June 1953.

W. A. Camwell

Plate 256: The 1896-built shed at Thornton in 1930, photographed only three years before closure when all of its engines and men were transferred to the new LNER shed at Thornton Junction. In amongst the NBR-built engines is an unidentifiable Class 04 engine, one of five such locomotives of that class allocated here during this period.

OPC Collection

Plate 257: Rife overcrowding at the old NBR shed at Thornton resulted in the LNER building this new shed at Thornton Junction in 1933. Some seventy locomotives were allocated to the old Thornton Shed in 1930, with room for only twenty, so the decision was taken to erect this corrugated iron clad building which closely followed former NBR shed designs. The six road through structure was complemented by a two road repair and lifting shop equipped with wheel drop, hoist and lathe, and in this June 1961 view the repair shop can be seen behind Class B1 4-6-0 No. 61343. Of course, with the new shed came facilities to match, with a 200 ton capacity twin bunker coaling plant, 70ft. turntable and a 150ft. long wet ash pit.

W. T. Stubbs

Plate 258: The east end of Thornton Junction in August 1952, with a handful of NBR-built engines on the yard. At this time there were in excess of a hundred locomotives on the allocation books, with former NBR types still in abundance alongside WD 2-8-0s and a couple of BR Standards.

D. F. Tee

Plate 259: All of the sheds depicted in this book were visited at one time or another over the years by hundreds, if not thousands, of railway enthusiasts. Indeed, most of the photographs illustrated were taken by some of those 'shed bashers'. This view shows, standing alongside Class J83 No. 68453 at Thornton Junction in May 1955, a man responsible for organising many of the Railway Correspondence & Travel Society visits to engine sheds during the BR period. No names are mentioned, but for those who may have memories of those visits, the gentleman in question resides in Nottingham, and has a colourful vocabulary.

Author's Collection

Plates 260 & 261: Two photographs of the Lancashire, Derbyshire & East Coast shed at Tuxford, taken before and after the Grouping. The upper view shows the shed and yard under GCR ownership, whilst the lower picture shows little change in either the 'northlight' shed or the allocation, only the numbers having changed and, of course, the weather.

W. H. Whitworth & F. Moore

Plate 262: The Raven-designed 3 cylinder Class T3s were the largest freight locomotives handed over by the NER at the Grouping and this view of No. 63462, by now designated Class Q7, shows off the massive bulk of these hard working engines. Seen here outside No. 1 Shed at Tyne Dock, in August 1954, the 0-8-0 shared the premises with the other fourteen members of its class, all of which had been allocated here since World War II for use on iron-ore trains to Consett.

B. Morrison

Plate 263: Two of the smaller residents, seen inside one of the roundhouses at Tyne Dock on the same day, were Class J25 0-6-0 No. 65694 and Class J72 0-6-0T No. 68743, both having stopped here for repairs. On the through turntable road can be seen one of the bogie hopper wagons used on the Tyne Dock to Consett iron-ore workings, that too being on shed for attention.

B. Morrison

Plate 264: Wearhead was the most westerly engine shed in County Durham, opening in 1895 when yet another branch line was completed by the North Eastern Railway. The tiny shed was home for the branch engine and in 1939 Class J21 0-6-0 No. 314 was the resident locomotive, its first working in this period being the morning 'down' train to Darlington. In the picture is No. 1561 of the same class, a Darlington engine which had worked the morning train in the opposite direction. The afternoon workings would, of course, balance the situation and bring No. 314 (later renumbered 65064) home to roost; a regular occurrence for the same locomotive until June 1953 when the shed closed.

C. A. Appleton

Plate 265:   Class J73 0-6-0T No. 68359 peeps through one of the brick arches of the straight road shed at West Hartlepool, in july 1956. In addition to this three road shed there were also two roundhouses adjacent to each other, sited at the southern end of the yard. The average allocation of West Hartlepool, during the LNER period, was 75 locomotives, mostly goods engines and a fair amount of tank engines. When it closed in September 1967, 51C, its code throughout the BR period, was amongst the last steam depots in the north-eastern area.

B. Morrison

Plate 266: A sunny day at Wigan, in June 1937, with two of the depot's dozen Class J10 0-6-0s outside the former MS&LR two road shed. Class J10s were allocated here until closure of the depot in 1952, by which time the establishment had come under the control of the London Midland Region of BR. The remaining examples of the class were sent to the nearby ex-LNWR shed at Springs Branch. Lower Ince, as the LNER's Wigan shed was known, was built at the end of the 1870s and had, as can be seen, typical period brick arch openings.

B. Hilton Collection

Plates 267 & 268 (right): Yet another of the GCR's London Extension depots was Woodford Halse, a six road dead end shed embodying all the standard features of the period. The top view shows the shed and yard in 1935, with plenty of GCR veterans in the picture. Below is the shed as it was in BR days, with a rebuilt roof and an annexe built on to the north-east corner of the shed for use by the newly-acquired diesel shunters. WD 2-8-0s formed the bulk of the depot's freight allocation, when this photograph was taken in August 1960, with nearly thirty of the class helping out the shed's Class B1 and K3 locomotives.

L & GRP/
Courtesy David & Charles & W. T. Stubbs

Plate 269:   Wrexham Shed, under new management, circa 1908. The former Wrexham, Mold & Connah's Quay Depot had been taken over by the GCR in 1905, and behind the antique locomotives can be seen the timber-built shed itself. In 1910, the new shed was partially destroyed in a fierce gale but two years later, a new brick-built six road engine shed was erected to replace it.

B. Hilton Collection

Plate 270:   Wrexham Motive Power Depot in 1950, again under new management but this time the last, although the shed still had ten years of life left before closure in January 1960. The transversed pitched roof of GCR design was holding up well to the rigours of the steam shed atmosphere, but just a few years after this photograph was taken disaster struck Wrexham again, and the first two bays of the roof were damaged, this time by fire. BR were quick to repair the damage, and rebuilt the roof to a near likeness of the GCR original.

B. Hilton

Plate 271: The M&GN shed at Yarmouth Beach had what is known as a twin 'Belfast' roof with glazed gables, and this view, taken in 1936, shows the unusual type of architecture employed, at least for engine sheds. To the left can be seen the small mechanical coaling plant, with a line of coal tubs awaiting more customers.

W. A. Camwell

Plate 272: By the time nationalisation came along, Yarmouth Beach had acquired a number of Class D2 4-4-0s of GNR origin, to replace withdrawn M&GN engines. No. 2152 was one of the Class D2s allocated to the resort, and is seen outside the shed in late 1948.

D. J. Montgomery

Plate 273: Yarmouth (South Town) was one of two GER engine sheds that were operational in this East Coast resort, the other shed, separated from South Town by the Yare Estuary, being sited at Vauxhall. Of the two, South Town always had the largest allocation, with anything from fifteen to twenty five locomotives, depending on the season, although the shed at Vauxhall was the larger building. In this 1931 view of South Town, Class D16/2 No. 8800, seen from ground level, looks menacingly large as it enjoys a Sunday rest with other members of its class.

G. Coltas

Plate 274: A pre-World War I interior view of a section of the NER shed at York North (Clifton), with an unidentified Lancashire & Yorkshire Railway Aspinall Class 2P 4-4-0 sharing stabling room with the resident NER engines. These are, from left to right, 398 class 0-6-0 No. 593, Tennant 2-4-0 No. 1475 and the youngster of the bunch, Class P2 0-6-0 No. 1678. From the earliest days of railways at York, a cosmopolitan atmosphere has existed, with foreign engines stabling anywhere amongst the numerous engine sheds which were to be found at this busy centre.

Author's Collection

Plate 275: Class J71 No. 68309 of Gateshead receives a wash-out at York, after arrival from the North in May 1959.

B. Morrison

Plate 276: A busy period at the north end of York Shed Yard in 1936, with the tracks giving the appearance of a switchback railway. The wagons were on the ash loading line which, as at most locations without mechanical loading equipment, ran at a lower level than the ash pit roads, simply to help yard staff with manual loading of the firebox debris. The track inclining upwards in front of the Class K3 locomotive, was the old coaling stage wagon ramp and was, by this time, defunct, all coaling being carried out by mechanical means.

Photomatic

CLOSED, SOLD OTHER USES, & DEMOLITION

Plate 277: The Great North of Scotland engine shed at Elgin was one of the last operational steam depots in Northern Scotland, closing in 1962 when steam was banished from that part of the country. After closure, the shed was used to store redundant diesel locomotives until it was taken over for private use. This view, taken in June 1963, shows the attractive stone-built shed with its transverse hipped roof, a design so popular north of the border.

W. T. Stubbs

Plate 278: The north end of Eastfield in August 1981, and although the type of motive power and the shed itself has changed dramatically, overcrowding is still a problem, although not quite as acute. The original NBR-designed steam shed was swept away in 1966, and this purpose-built diesel repair and maintenance depot was erected in its place. Fourteen years of diesel exhausts had even managed to darken the lightweight corrugated wall cladding. Compare this view with *Plate 134*.

J. A. Sommerfield

Plate 279: The site of Denaby Shed, near Mexborough, in the late 1930s, with three 'pilgrims' standing on what was the floor of the former H&BR timber-built shed. The rear half of the 115ft. long single-pitched roof engine house was damaged by fire in July 1921 but it was rebuilt, only to close in May 1927. Its only occupants, Class J23 0-6-0 No. 2461 and Class N12 0-6-0T No. 2489, were sent away to Cudworth and Dairycoates respectively. The 50ft. turntable was left in situ, and was regularly used until BR days.

W. A. Camwell

Plate 280: A garden of remembrance, or the ultimate accolade, on the site of the former GER engine shed at Enfield Town, in June 1981. The shed, built in 1872, was closed in November 1960 and demolished shortly afterwards, the grimy havens of the steam locomotive having no useful purpose on the modern electric railway.

J. A. Sommerfield

Plates 281 & 282: Demolition of Borough Gardens in progress during July 1960, some thirteen months after closure. This large former NER shed contained four turntables, the original part of the shed opening in 1875 and containing two 42ft. 6in. diameter turntables, each with 24 radiating roads. By the turn of the century, the shed was doubled in length and a further two turntables were laid, increasing the shed's stabling capacity to 92 locomotives. The allocation consisted mainly of freight locomotives, with Class Q6 0-8-0s forming the bulk of the tender locomotives during the LNER period. The sheer size of these multi-table roundhouses rendered them virtually useless for further industrial use once the steam engines had left, so most were razed to the ground. Once demolition was complete, the Borough Gardens site was taken up by a new freight depot serving the Tyneside area.

W. T. Stubbs

Plate 283: Borough Gardens in August 1961. Twelve months after the two previous views were taken, the roof has gone and only the walls remain. The pits of the radiating roads and the turntable pits are still there to remind us, but not for long.

J. A. Sommerfield

Plate 284: With the coming of diesel traction to the former LNER territory in the late 1950s, plans were drawn up to build new sheds purely for use by the new form of motive power, but in some cases, with various alterations and some modification, certain steam locomotive sheds were found to be ideal for diesel use. One such shed was Gateshead, where the former NER roundhouse had received a new roof in the mid-1950s. It was found that by taking out the turntables and associated radiating roads, and putting in nine straight roads across the full width of the shed, a large modern diesel servicing and repair shed was created for part of the cost of a completely new building of only half the size. This June 1964 view of Gateshead shows the transformation virtually complete, with diesel traction already installed.

W. T. Stubbs

Plates 285 & 286:   The first engine shed erected at Stratford was this polygonal roundhouse, built by the GER in the early 1840s. The shed had sixteen stabling roads, including entry/exit roads, and served as a running shed until 1888 when the whole of the locomotive running department moved across the main line to what was then known as the 'Jubilee' Shed. In addition to this roundhouse, there was also a four road straight shed built just behind, and physically joined to, the round shed. Both buildings were absorbed into the Stratford Works complex and saw use for many years, the straight shed as a paint shop and the round shed as a wheel shop. The upper view, showing off well the work's setting, was taken in 1946 and the lower internal shot, taken at the same time, shows the shed during a quiet period.

British Rail

Plate 287: Two months after closure, and the weeds are already getting a grip at Stockton.

W. T. Stubbs

Plate 288: The remains of Leicester (Belgrave Road), pictured in April 1957. This former GNR 'northlight'-roofed shed was opened in 1882 and, for most of its existence, was a sub-shed of Colwick although during some of the BR period, it was under the supervision of the ex-GCR depot at Leicester. Closure came in 1956.

J. Bateman

Plate 289: The ex-H&BR running shed at Bullcroft Junction was, like Denaby and Hull (Alexandra Dock) sheds, built from timber, an obvious cost saving measure when they were erected in the 1880s. The trouble was that timber sheds were liable to deteriorate far quicker than their brick-built counterparts, and the ever-present danger of fire could wreak havoc in minutes. As events turned out Bullcroft escaped these two most serious of disasters, but its life was short, the shed being closed by the end of 1931. In the last months of operational use the shed housed two 4-8-0 tanks, a Class J23, a Class N12 and a Class 04. Demolition followed some years after closure.

W. A. Camwell

Plate 290: Doncaster, on 24th May 1970, and just as is stands today with the whole of the shed still utilised by the BR standard diesel classes. Although the relics of steam such as turntables, coaling facilities and ash plants are gone, the depot remains unchanged. No longer is there a dark smoke haze hanging above the shed, a location aid that helped so many of us on our first visits to any steam shed. The allocation of Doncaster is now but a handful of Class 08 diesel shunters, as these Class 47 and 31 main line diesels are only stabling for the weekend. It is a far cry from the days when this depot had 200 plus locomotives on its books, many of them representing the 'glamour' classes of East Coast Main Line steam power. But at least Doncaster has not yet suffered the indignity of full closure and demolition unlike Grantham, King's Cross and New England.

J. A. Sommerfield

Plate 291: Mallaig, in use as a fish box store in 1980. This is one of the less attractive uses for an old engine shed, at least as far as the nose is concerned.

J. A. Sommerfield

Plate 292: Durham, in July 1960, eighteen months after closure. This shed was opened by the NER in 1864 to house four engines of the day, but an extension was added to the rear at an unknown date. In the early LNER period, tender engines of Classes J21 and J22 were to be found allocated here but by 1930, four Class G5 0-4-4Ts became the permanent motive power, with Nos. 7263, 7285, 7298 and 7307 seeing the shed through to BR ownership. For the last twelve months of its operational life, Durham was home for three of the massive Class A8 Pacific tank engines.

W. T. Stubbs

Shortly after St. Margaret's Motive Power Depot was closed in April 1967, one enterprising Scottish railway enthusiast, by the name of A. A. 'Sandy' Maclean, carried out a photographic survey of the buildings and yards that comprised this large Edinburgh shed. This had the effect of capturing scenes that had not been possible before, because of the presence of the steam locomotive. The following four plates are a selection from that survey, and the author hopes they will bring back memories to those who remember the atmosphere of a shed when the steam locomotive had left for ever.

Plate 293 (above): The roofless six road straight shed and yard with, on the right, the 300ft. long single-sided coaling stage.

Plate 294 (below): Looking across the main line, to the site of the now demolished tank roundhouse.

Plate 295: The sand furnace, outside the stone-built straight shed.

Plate 296: No smoke, steam or pollution, just emptiness and silence in the servicing yard. The inclined road in the centre held the wagons which were used to cart away the depot's ashes. The 70ft. turntable, installed in 1943, was sited just out of picture to the right. The one road, brick-built repair shop was also of LNER vintage.

Plates 297 & 298: Opened in early 1867 by the NER, Tebay was a typical 'period' stone-built shed, with arched openings for the engine roads and twin-pitched roofs. The building held eight engines and, as was usual with most remote junction depots, houses were provided for enginemen and their families. The depot apparently closed for a short period in the 1870s but, by 1878, there were eight 0-6-0 tender locomotives stationed there. At the end of October 1902, the establishment was closed and, when necessary, NER engines used the LNWR shed. These two views of the engine shed in its closed state show *(upper)* the building in the 1930s, still very much complete, and *(lower)* the roofless shed in May 1948.

W. A. Camwell & D. F. Tee

Plate 299: St. Helens not only boasted an engine shed of LNWR origin at Sutton Oak, but it also had this small shed, of MS&LR origin, on the north side of the town which, by early 1937, was in this state of disuse and dereliction.
W. A. Camwell

Plate 300: The closed engine shed at Whitby, on 24th August 1977, 130 years after it was built by the York & North Midland Railway. The original 1847 building was slightly smaller, but extensions carried out by the NER brought the shed up to this size. Closed in April 1959, the shed had been home for some of the largest NER-built tank engines as well as numerous 0-6-0s, from Classes J22 to J27, but its last residents were three LMS-designed 2-6-4 tank engines and a couple of BR Standard 2-6-0 tender engines.
J. A. Sommerfield

Plate 301: Although Battersby was closed by the NER in 1895, the shed remained intact until 1965 when demolition finally took place. This 1930s view shows the shed in remarkably good condition, but this is understandable when, in fact, steam locomotives only used the place for no more than ten years in all. Opened in early 1877, the shed closed after only a few years but was reopened in 1889, only to close again six years later. No doubt, when it was open, it never saw a full house as the traffic from the area did not materialise as expected, and only a handful of engines sheltered under its roof. The tracks leading into the building were lifted in the late 1920s, after it had previously been used to store withdrawn engines and, during World War I, dining saloons of the East Coast Joint stock.

W. A. Camwell

Plate 302: March Whitemoor Shed in July 1976, 13 years after steam engines had left. This shed was classed as the wash-out shed and the large boiler house used in conjunction with the process, can be seen alongside, cold and silent. After the departure of steam locomotives, this shed was used for wagon storage for a number of years.

J. A. Sommerfield

Plate 303: Gorton roundhouse was built in 1848, closed in 1879, absorbed in 1880, closed again in 1963 and demolished in 1965. This was all that remained of the unique Manchester, Sheffield & Lincolnshire Railway roundhouse at Gorton in November 1965, after the demolition crews had been given the blessing of 'official' vandals. This shed is well described in George Dow's book *Great Central (Volume One)*, and it would surely have been a candidate for preservation had not the authorities decided otherwise. Admittedly the 40ft. diameter turntable, with its two off centre tracks, had been scrapped when the building was absorbed into the Gorton Works complex in 1880, to become an iron foundry but, essentially, the building was intact with all its original components. The roof, as can be seen, was a mass of girders and tie-bars, all resting on the single central column. So progress marches on, as it did at Gorton and Openshaw in the 1960s when, as well as this event, the whole railway complex comprising running sheds, locomotive, carriage and wagon shops were torn down to make way for a new wholesale vegetable market. So ended 120 years of railway history, in a part of Manchester that owed so much to the iron horse.

W. A. Brown

Acknowledgements

Compiling this album of LNER engine shed views has been a great pleasure, although sometimes made difficult by the fact that I have had to leave out so much good material simply because there wasn't enough room. Many people have helped by supplying photographs taken by their own cameras, while others have allowed me to sort through their collections, giving me complete freedom and, at the same time, passing on to me the hospitality that seems to be so much a part of our hobby. Certain names crop up that were included in the *LMS Sheds in Camera*, and to these gentlemen I say 'thank you again'. The publishers of this book have helped with my many enquiries and requests, and two people deserve a mention for putting up with my incessant and impatient phone calls and letters, Geoffrey Charters and Jill Cottom. Last of all, my good lady, Christine, who has endured endless hours of me 'doing the book'. To all of you, many thanks.

Alex Appleton	Alec George	George Reeve
Paul Bolger	A. R. Goult	Allan Sommerfield
Alan Brown	Brian Green	Bill Stubbs
Bill Camwell	Roger Griffiths	Dave Swales
Hubert Casserley	Chris Hawkins	Peter Tatlow
Gordon Coltas	Brian Hilton	Nelson Twells
Ron Dyer	A. A. Maclean	British Rail Eastern Region
John Edgington	Bernard Matthews	National Railway Museum
The late George Ellis	David Montgomery	Nottingham County Library Service
Ken Fairey	Brian Morrison	Photomatic
Vic Forster	Bill Potter	West Yorkshire Records Office

Index To Plates

Aberdeen (Ferryhill) 71, 72
Alloa 73, 74
Alnmouth 75, 76
Alston 77
Annesley 78, 79, 80
Ardsley 17, 81

Ballater 82, 83
Bathgate 19, 84
Battersby 301
Berwick 85
Bidston 86, 87, 88
Borough Gardens 89, 281, 282, 283
Bowes Bridge 90
Braintree 91
Breakdown Cranes 48-56
Bridlington 92
Brunswick 47, 93, 94, 95
Bullcroft Junction 289
Burntisland 96
Bury St. Edmunds 97

Cambridge 32
Carlisle (Canal) 98
Chester (Northgate) 99, 100
Colchester 101, 102, 103
Colwick 43, 104-108
Consett 109, 110
Copley Hill 111, 112
Cudworth 113, 114

Darlington (Bank Top) 66, 115-118
Darlington (North Road) 119
Darnall 14, 15, 31, 36, 41, 61, 120, 121
Denaby 279
Dinting 122
Doncaster 123-127, 290
Dundee (Tay Bridge) 128, 129
Dunfermline 68, 130-133
Durham 292

Eastfield 21, 64, 134-138, 278
East Hartlepool 139
Elgin 277
Enfield Town 280

Ferryhill 140
Fort William 141
Frodingham 2-13, 38, 59, 142, 143

Gateshead 46, 144-147, 284
Gorton 34, 148-155, 303
Grantham 63, 156, 157, 158

Hatfield 44, 45
Haverton Hill 159

Hayfield 160
Haymarket 60, 161-165
Heaton 166
Heaton Mersey 26, 167
Hitchin 168
Hornsey 169
Hull (Alexandra Dock) 170
Hull (Botanic Gardens) 62
Hull (Springhead) 171

Ilford 172
Immingham 173, 174, 175
Ipswich 69, 176, 177

Keadby 18
Keith 178
King's Cross Station Yard 28, 57, 67, 179
King's Cross Top Shed 29, 180, 181
Kirkby Stephen 182
Kittybrewster 30, 183, 184

Langwith Junction 39, 185, 186
Leicester GC 20, 187
Leicester GN 288
Leyburn 188
Lincoln GC 189
Loch Leven 190

Mallaig 191, 192, 291
March (Whitemoor) 16, 35, 193, 302
Melton Constable 194
Mexborough 195, 196
Middlesbrough 197
Middleton-in-Teesdale 198
Montrose 199

Neasden 1, 200
Neville Hill 70
New England 25, 37, 201-211
New Holland 212
Northallerton 213
North Berwick 214
Northwich 215
Norwich (City) 216, 217
Norwich (Thorpe) 218, 219
Nottingham (Arkwright Street) 220

Parkhead 221
Parkeston Quay 222
Pateley Bridge 223
Penistone 224
Perth 225
Pickering 27
Polmont 40, 226, 227

Reedsmouth 228
Retford (GCR) 230, 231
Retford (GNR) 42
Riccarton Junction 229

St. Helens 299
St. Margaret's 232-238, 293-296
Scarborough 58, 239, 240
Selby 241, 242
Southport 243, 244
Starbeck 245
Staveley 22, 246-249
Stockton 250, 287
Stratford 23, 24, 251, 252, 253, 285, 286
Sunderland 254

Tebay 297, 298
Thaxted 255
Thornton 256
Thornton Junction 257, 258, 259
Tuxford 260, 261
Tyne Dock 262, 263

Wearhead 264
West Hartlepool 265
Whitby 300
Wigan 266
Woodford 267, 268
Wrexham 269, 270

Yarmouth (Beach) 271, 272
Yarmouth (South Town) 273
York 33, 65, 274, 275, 276